HIDDEN
HISTORY
of
YPSILANTI

Laura Bien

Charleston · London

THE
History
PRESS

Published by The History Press
Charleston, SC 29403
www.historypress.net

Images courtesy of the Ypsilanti Archives and the author's collection.

First published 2011

Manufactured in the United States

ISBN 978.1.60949.289.2

Bien, Laura.
Hidden history of Ypsilanti / Laura Bien
p. cm.
ISBN 978-1-60949-289-2
1. Ypsilanti (Mich.)--History. 2. Ypsilanti (Mich.)--Social life and customs. 3. Ypsilanti (Mich.)--Politics and government. 4. Ypsilanti (Mich.)--Biography. 5. Food habits--Michigan--Ypsilanti--History. 6. Women--Michigan--Ypsilanti--History. 7. Women employees--Michigan--Ypsilanti--History. 8. Inventions--Michigan--Ypsilanti--History. 9. Household employees--Michigan--Ypsilanti--History. I. Title.
F574.Y8B59 2011
977.4'35--dc23
2011033503

For Fritz.

CONTENTS

CONTENTS

FOREWORD

In Laura Bien's first book, *Tales of the Ypsilanti Archives*, she gave the historic buildings in Ypsilanti a voice to tell their stories. In her latest book, *Hidden History of Ypsilanti*, Bien recounts long-forgotten stories about Ypsilanti food, politics, inventors and women. She provides her readers with the full details of Ypsilanti's only nineteenth-century female photographer, how Model T cars were converted into ice saws and why a Ford Lake fish kill went bad in the early 1970s, among many other stories.

Bien's tales are both entertaining and cautionary. Their lesson: the simple life was not always so simple. Before we look ahead to the future, perhaps a quick glance back to the past may offer us some guidance. Laura Bien's *Hidden History of Ypsilanti* allows us that quick glance back.

Paul Schreiber
Mayor
Ypsilanti, Michigan

PREFACE

A tour guide in Michigan's second-largest contiguous historic district could point out examples of Second Empire, Queen Anne, Italianate, Romanesque, Gothic Revival and other architectural styles. However beautiful, the mansards, quoins, turrets, towers, stucco and slate reveal little about the onetime lives behind the front doors. Rather than a curbside view of exterior splendor, this book attempts to give the reader a humbler, yet more intimate, invitation to dinner.

Stories in "A Different Dining Room" examine forgotten foodways and local food companies. "Out of the Kitchen" offers a chronological set of portraits of local women in the workforce and women's social movements. "Late Night in the Workshop" collects tales of overlooked inventions and technology. "Servants' Quarters" explores the little-chronicled lives of domestic servants. "The Neighborhood" takes a look at wider issues in town, and "Leaving Home" examines the little-known lives of Ypsilantians who left one world to find another.

Grateful thanks are due to Patricia Majher of *Michigan History* magazine, Dave Askins and Mary Morgan of the *Ann Arbor Chronicle*, Austen Smith of the *Ypsilanti Courier* and Steve Pierce of *YpsiNews.com*, in whose publications' pages these stories originally appeared. Ruth Van Stee at the Grand Rapids Public Library, Preservation Eastern director Deirdre Fortino and Ypsilanti Archives assistant director Derek Spinei kindly found and shared elusive images. Eastern Michigan University (EMU) electronic media and film lecturer Matthew Hanson shared a tip that developed into a story about cartoonist Winsor McCay. Cumberland County Historical Society member

Barbara Landis shared crucial information about onetime Carlisle School student George Moore. Muskegon's Lakeshore Museum Center staff members enriched my heretofore scanty knowledge about earth closets. The Ypsilanti Archives' own "Cadaver Dog," George Ridenour, scanned many never-before-published glass negatives, some of which appear here. Thanks are also due to our honorable Mayor Schreiber, the staff of the Ypsilanti Archives and, most of all, to readers with whom I am privileged to take a look behind the front door.

Part I

A Different Dining Room

The Little Condiment Company

Once upon a time, the Huron was a saltwater river, but not for long—neither a long time nor a long distance. The time was an occasional half hour once a week or so during the last decade of the nineteenth century. The distance was just a few yards, on the east side of the stream just south of Cross Street bridge.

Those salty waters may have included a green cucumber pickle or two, floating downstream to Belleville and possibly on to Lake Erie. If a fisherman there wondered about the lake-faring gherkin, he likely wouldn't have guessed that it came from the immense pickling vats of Depot Town's onetime brinery, a curious spot from which pungent odors wafted all over Depot Town.

Imagine, instead, that Lake Erie pickle on an Ypsilanti turn-of-the-century dinner table—for that is where its story begins. If modern-day diners tried a local meal in 1900, they might find it bland. Ypsilanti private and commercial kitchens of this era lacked the well-stocked, and often multiethnic, spice racks of today.

A peek inside an 1899 recipe book collected by Ann Arbor's Congregational Church, for example, reveals that in a sample of more than 140 recipes, the vast majority are seasoned with only salt and pepper. Very few dishes incorporated other spices, including (in descending order) parsley, cayenne, nutmeg, mace, bay leaf and sage. Conspicuous in their absence are such spices as oregano, thyme, cilantro and basil—not to mention more recent and exotic choices like adobo and lemongrass.

The turn-of-the-century Ypsilanti household, however, had another option for livening up meals. Popular table condiments included a variety of pickled vegetable relishes like piccalilli and chow chow. Sometimes served from fancy condiment containers, the savory garnishes added flavor and zest.

In about 1892, three enterprising Ypsi men decided to cash in on this food fashion. They founded the tiny Ypsilanti Condiment Company in Depot Town. Two of the company founders were the sons of successful local businessmen. President James Deubel helped his father, William, operate the Deubel flour mill on the north side of Cross Street, just east of the river. Condiment company secretary and treasurer Charles Ferrier was also secretary and treasurer for his father Philo's Machine Works company (now the Ypsilanti Food Coop). Alexander Fee joined the men as a worker.

The men built a 150- by 10-foot building, aligned east to west, behind what is now the City Body auto shop. On the east side of the building stood ten enormous pickling vats, each one nine feet wide and several feet tall. Soon the shipments of vegetables began arriving, and pickling got underway.

The vats' briny aromas mingled with the equine scents from three nearby Depot Town stables then standing, each one about ten feet from the Ypsilanti Condiment Company (the era's sanitation awareness left something to be desired). The western half of the condiment company's narrow building held a storage area for supplies and crates of vegetables.

The Ypsilanti Condiment Company produced chili sauce, "table sauce," piccalilli, chow chow, catsup, pickled olives, pickled vegetables and pickled

An 1897 ad for the Depot Town company displayed its savory sundries. *Author's collection.*

pickles. One early customer was the state boys' reform school in Lansing. In the summer of 1892, the school ordered a barrel of pickles, a dozen pints of chow chow and another dozen pints of catsup.

It was only one of many orders beginning to come in from throughout the state. The little condiment company seemed to have a bright and briny future. Just four years later, however, another bottle of catsup got the company in trouble.

This particular bottle had been purchased in Manistee by a state food inspector. In 1896, food safety laws hadn't yet been passed on the federal level. Michigan, like other states, had already passed its own state-level food purity laws. This was out of necessity—counterfeit and adulterated food was a major problem of the day.

"The conditions of the stocks of food products at the time of the commencement of our work was simply frightful," wrote state inspector W.B. Scattergood in his 1896 report. Chief among adulterated foods were coffee, spices, fruit jams and jellies, milk, butter, candy and vinegar. Michigan inspectors fanned out across the state each year and collected samples to bring to Lansing for analysis.

One such lab sample was a dab of catsup from the Ypsilanti Condiment Company. Chief inspector C.E. Storrs found that it contained salicylic acid, a common food preservative of the day. The condiment company was censured by inclusion in the state food bureau's annual report for 1896. It was the only Ypsi company to be listed that year (only a small handful of other Ypsi companies were cited through the years).

The shame of the citation didn't last too long; two years later, the company was caught again, this time for tainted cider vinegar. The incident seemed to presage a similar souring of the company's luck.

Soon after the turn of the century, the little condiment company went out of business. The enormous pickling vats drained their last salty dregs into the river. The vats were removed. The gherkins were gone.

By 1909, the company's long, narrow building had been converted to a big stable as part of J.E. Engel's coal, wood and horse teaming business. In time, that business faded away as horses became obsolete. The onetime condiment company's building was razed.

Today, a walk down Photo Street brings the explorer within arm's reach of the long-vanished building and within earshot of the river's splashing current. The vats are long empty, the structure is gone and only yellowed maps still record the city's onetime distributor of dubious delicacies and purveyor of purity-challenged pickles.

It's forgivable to shed a salty tear.

AS THE COFFEE GRINDER TURNS

At a recent antique show at the Washtenaw Farm Council Grounds, my husband and I bought a cute wood and copper coffee grinder. "Cool; I can do it like they did it in the nineteenth century!" I thought.

At home, I poured store-bought roasted beans into the grinder's cup and turned the handle. Fifteen minutes later, I was still turning. The following morning, I tried to "Tom Sawyer" the kitchen chore onto my husband. "Try it! It's pretty fun!" I enthused, sidling back to the still-toasty bed. Within a week, the grinder was occupying a space in my collection of copper kettles atop the fridge, and we'd returned to using the good old can of ground coffee from Meijer. We gave up on the related idea of attempting to home-roast the beans. Phew.

Yet between 1867 and 1882, thirteen different home coffee roasters were patented in Michigan, seven of them in Ypsilanti. One Ypsilanti manufactory shipped several different models nationwide and employed a traveling salesman to sniff out new markets.

The popularity of coffee roasters around the 1870s could be attributed to the coffee distributors' greed, ingenuity and deceit. In Michigan's early days of pioneer privation, raw coffee beans could be roasted in a cast-iron pan or Dutch oven. Whether in the hearth or on the stove, the method didn't work very well, resulting in uneven roasting and burnt beans.

It didn't work too well for Michigan soldiers in the Civil War either, who received rations of unripe beans. The men roasted their coffee beans in camp kettles. Some made small pans by removing the circumferential lead solder from a canteen.

"In Civil War re-enacting, coffee, prepared from raw beans, fire roasted and ground in a cloth bag smashed between a rifle butt and a rock, is the authentic method used when serious hardcore preparation is called for," noted local reenactor John Delcamp in a personal e-mail. "Although not a coffee drinker, I completely enjoyed my cup from the captain's kettle one frosty morning. It was the only thing available to drink, and I was thankful to get it."

Roasting and smashing the beans was laborious, but few 1860s soldiers would willingly forsake their cup of coffee. Some were tasting the beverage for the first time.

After the war, those new coffee drinkers and their fellow soldiers returned home. As trade across the reunified country normalized, the demand for coffee grew. Some local households purchased labor-saving preroasted and preground coffee in paper sacks. There was only one problem with that. It was a big one, but not a new one.

"Look Out For Ground Coffee," warned the October 16, 1843 issue of *Michigan Farmer and Western Agriculturalist* magazine:

> *Our readers are probably some of them aware that coffee packed in papers, and ready for immediate use, is offered at many of the groceries and shops of the dealers in such articles. Occasionally a good article may be offered; but to show of what a large portion of this ready made coffee is made, we make the following extract from the London Shipping List. "It has been ascertained that sawdust from mahogany, to the amount of more than 800 tons, has been used in the adulteration of what is called ready prepared coffee."*

Sawdust was but one of myriad substances used to adulterate coffee. Roasted peas, chicory, acorns, corn and grains were blended in, sometimes in excess of 75 percent of the mixture's volume, minimizing the actual coffee content and maximizing profits. In Michigan, adulterated ground coffee became the norm and pure coffee a rarity.

One University of Michigan pharmacy student, Ypsilantian Samuel Crombie, put eight samples of ground coffee he'd purchased from local shops under his microscope. He examined the cellular structures of the samples, sketched them and compared them to the actual cellular structure of coffee. His findings were published in the September 1882 issue of Ann Arbor–based *Physician and Surgeon* magazine.

Samuel examined Centennial Coffee, Gillie's Gold Medal Java and ground coffee bought in bulk. All, without exception, were adulterated. Gillie's, he said, "contained but very little coffee and was composed of wheat in great quantities, much of it unground, [as well as] chicory, corn, and peas."

He continued: "Inquiry was made and in every case investigation showed that there is but very little sale for coffee in any other form than in the unground berry, it being very generally recognized that coffee put upon the market in packages or in the ground form is almost certain to contain adulterations, and the fact that only eight of over thirty stores visited keep it on sale is evidence that there is very little demand for it."

Roasting beans at home was still an imperfect solution. Into this breach stepped Ypsilantian Cassius Hall, the single most prolific coffee roaster/inventor in Michigan history.

Born in Michigan in 1847, Cassius invented his first coffee roaster at age twenty-eight. It was a simple pot whose base fit into one of a cast-iron stovetop's normally lidded holes. Inside the pot was a horizontal wire mesh cylinder whose axial rod was supported at each end in grooves in the pot's rim, with a handle at one end of the rod. Coffee beans placed in the cylinder could be rotated in the hot air rising from the stove.

Cassius was granted a patent for his roaster in March 1876. His employer, Parsons Brothers, began producing and shipping his roasters. Cassius did not rest on his laurels. Over the next four years, he patented four increasingly sophisticated iterations of his roaster, culminating in his masterpiece. It

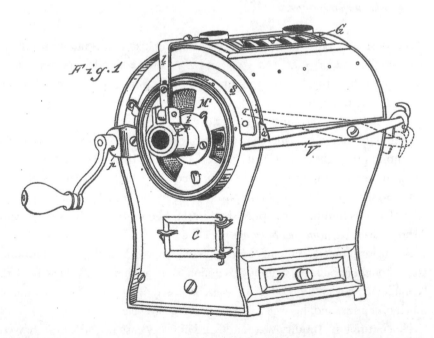

Cassius Hall invented increasingly sophisticated coffee roasters, culminating in this model in 1880. *Author's collection.*

featured an enclosed heating system, a sort of Archimedes screw to move the beans back and forth and a tilting chamber that poured the roasted beans neatly out. His employer advertised the device as the "Peerless."

One of Cassius's inventions doubled as a peanut roaster, and other Michigan-created roasters did double or triple duty. Daniel Denison of Troy invented a coffee roaster that also popped corn. George Merrick of Adrian created one that roasted coffee and peanuts and popped corn. Mathias Stein of Ypsilanti outdid them all with an intricate and fussy contraption that claimed to simultaneously roast coffee and heat sadirons. Mathias kept his day job as a cigar-maker.

As coffee roasters became more commonplace in 1870s homes, the market for ground coffee, as Crombie had noted in 1882, dwindled. Coffee merchants, however, devised a new gambit to boost sales, borrowing a trick from across the pond, where one practice had a history so pervasive that laws were passed against it.

In 1891, an enterprising Philadelphia manufacturer began mailing samples of his product to grocers.

Dear Sir:

Herewith we present for your inspection a sample of coffee compound.
It contains nothing but the best of pure and healthful ingredients, and is made only in the bean shape.
By blending with the natural coffee bean you can improve it, and bring it within the reach of those unable to purchase at the present high price of coffee.
…In ordering, send sample of roast, so that we can match your goods…

Yours, etc.,
The Dowling MFG. Co.

The Dowling beans were made of glucose, water and rye flour mixed into a paste, pressed into a mold and then dried and roasted. Some counterfeiters made fake beans in machines that resembled nineteenth-century candy machines.

Another bogus bean maker wrote:

Dear Sir:

I send you by this mail a sample of "imitation coffee."
This is a manufactured bean, and composed of flour; you can easily mix 15 per cent of this substitute in with genuine coffee that ranges in price from 20 to 22 cents, and it will improve the flavor of the same; it granulates the same as coffee. If you deal with us it will be in the most strict confidence.
…By the use of our bean you can increase your profits to 11 cents per pound and improve the flavor…

Yours,
L.H. Hall

[P.S.] I would not show samples even to employees.

A *New York Tribune* article reprinted in the December 4, 1886 *Scientific American* had this to say:

Years ago, all the coffee was ground in the grocery, but adulteration was carried on so extensively that the practice was established of buying the whole bean. This led some inventive Yankee humanitarian, who believed that too much coffee is bad for the nerves, to bring out the flour bean.
The grocer is not a foolish man. He does not sell these flour beans for coffee. This would give the business away. But when trade is dull, and the grocer must have something to occupy his mind, it is a pleasant recreation for him to mix a quantity of the flour beans with the genuine coffee. Then it cannot be easily detected. Only just enough of the flavorless bean is used to make a little profit. This is not quite one-half. When the honest housewife who buys whole coffee so as to get it pure grinds up this mixture, and the odor steals out from the mill, her eyes snap, and she laughs at the people who are foolish enough to buy the coffee which is ground at the store, and can be easily adulterated.

Finally, Michiganders had had enough. In 1895, the state passed an act "to prohibit and prevent adulteration, fraud, and deception in the manufacture and sale of articles of food and drink." The act mandated that items marketed as butter, cheese, lard, liquor, fruit jelly, butter, canned fruits and vegetables or coffee beans be pure and clearly labeled.

Michigan's pure foods act predated by eleven years the federal Pure Food and Drug Act of 1906. Adulterated foods continued to appear for a while in Michigan after both sets of legislation. But the era of labor-intensive coffee made from bogus beans faded away soon after.

The Golden Age of Oysters

After the 2010 Gulf oil spill, numerous restaurants pulled oysters from the menu.

The nation's oldest continually operating oyster-shucking company, New Orleans's P&J's, shut down. Nearby stands French Quarter neighbor Antoine's, New Orleans's oldest restaurant that allegedly invented the sumptuous dish Oysters Rockefeller. The restaurant has kept the recipe secret to this day.

More obvious was the fact that restaurants around the country that relied on Gulf oysters were in trouble. According to NOAA, the Gulf supplied about 67 percent of the nation's oysters.

Closer to home but further in time, oysters came from a different coast. Packed in barrels and whisked from New York and Chesapeake Bay to Washtenaw on trains more than 150 years ago, oysters were a popular area food.

Some were unloaded from the Ypsi train depot in the 1840s and hauled to the Oyster Saloon, owned by George Collins. His ad in the May 26, 1846 *Ypsilanti Sentinel* noted that "his stock of Tea, Coffee, Sugar, Molasses, Confectionaries, &c. &c. far surpasses any thing in the market. He has also fitted up a convenient Oyster Saloon adjoining his store, where he is prepared to serve the lovers of this luxury to the utmost of their wishes."

Oyster saloons in general ranged from opulent dining palaces to less elaborate eateries and even dives associated with gambling and prostitution. The menu usually included raw, stewed, broiled and fried oysters.

Ypsilanti's James Forsyth expanded this model with his 1859 Oyster and Billiard Saloon on Huron between Pearl Street and Michigan Avenue. Local papers ran ads for Detroit oyster packer D.D. Mallory and the Oyster Ocean restaurant at Woodward and Jefferson Avenues, which presumably

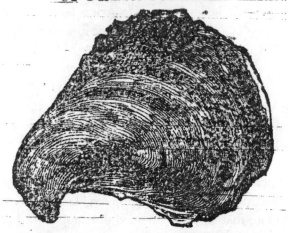

D. D. MALLORY & CO.

PACKERS OF THE CELEBRATED

DIAMOND BRAND

OF FRESH OYSTERS.

FRUITS and VEGETABLES.
Wholesale and Retail
Dealers in FOREIGN and DOMESTIC FRUITS.
68 Jefferson Ave., DETROIT.
757w4

Detroit oyster packers and restaurants advertised in Ypsilanti papers. *Author's collection.*

served the bivalve. In the 1860s, Depot Town grocer W.K. Horner stocked mackerel, salmon, lobster and live oysters.

Customers who wished to cook them at home were given their deshelled purchase in a paper oyster pail. Numerous inventors filed patents for such paper containers for oysters in the late nineteenth and early twentieth centuries. When oyster stocks declined and takeout food became more popular some time after World War II, the unused stocks of paper oyster pails were adopted for takeout. Today's standard Chinese takeout comes in cardboard oyster-pails.

Outside of home, oyster suppers were a popular local form of social dining for years. Often held in a church and combined with entertainment, the suppers were frequently fundraisers. Diners could usually choose from a variety of oyster dishes, but oyster stew was a mainstay.

"The Wesleyan Guild of the Methodist church gives a novel entertainment in the church parlors next Monday evening," reported the January 18, 1889

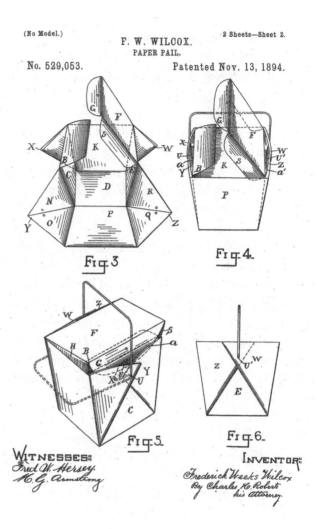

(No Model.) · 2 Sheets—Sheet 2.

F. W. WILCOX.
PAPER PAIL.

No. 529,053.   Patented Nov. 13, 1894.

In 1894, F.W. Wilcox invented one form of the paper oyster pail still used today. *Author's collection.*

Ann Arbor Argus. "It is to be a 'Conversazione' where, to the music of the Chequamegons [local orchestra] five minute conversations will be enjoyed, on topics assigned by the program. An oyster supper is promised. Admission fee of 10 cents [$2.40 in 2011 dollars]."

Everyone liked oysters, it seemed. However, one well-known Michigan man stood up against the mollusk. Former EMU and University of Michigan (UM) student J. Harvey Kellogg took a dim view of oysters. In a talk he gave to the state horticultural society in 1907, Kellogg brought the gavel down, describing a banquet he had attended:

The first thing on the bill of fare was oysters. I did not want any. Why?

In the first place, the oyster is a scavenger; his business is to lick off the slime at the bottom of the sea; you catch the oyster down there; he has got his broad lips open and licking off the slime; he likes that slime because it is full of germs.

Lemon juice will kill not only oyster germs, but typhoid fever germs. Oyster germs are typhoid fever germs. That is why people get typhoid fever sometimes by eating raw oysters. If you are fond of typhoid fever germs, oysters on the half shell will be a good way to get them. The oyster lives largely on typhoid fever germs. He likes them. You can almost always find typhoid fever germs in oyster stomachs.

At the time, Kellogg was hosting the state horticultural society at his Battle Creek Sanitarium for the meeting, which included a dinner. The menu at the "San" banquet included roasted Protose, a meat substitute made of beans blended with peanut butter. Other delectables included "Nut and Rice Croquettes" and "Wafers," all washed down with "NoKo."

A 1909 advertisement in the *Ypsilanti Daily Press* showed a gentleman who apparently did not ascribe to the austere Kellogg diet. The ad touted the "Sealshipt" method of packing oyster meats in a sanitary can. The company even offered a book about its method, should the ad's reader be intrigued. The ad listed three Ypsilanti grocers who carried the trademark white china crock from which the oyster meats were dipped into a take-home container. The ad also showed the item of cutlery designed just for oysters: the dainty bident oyster fork. Also manufactured were oyster plates, with a set of depressions in which to nestle the half-shells.

The age of oysters, however, was slowly coming to a close. Over the course of the 1900s, oyster stocks dwindled, and the food became more expensive. In November 1931, the delicacy was well out of reach of most Depression-era budgets. That month, Ypsilanti's elegant Huron Hotel included them in one of its weekly Sunday dinners. However, the oyster was no longer the main dish as at past oyster suppers. The hotel's entrees included grilled Mackinac trout, fried veal porterhouse, baked chicken and filet mignon. Oysters appeared merely as an "oyster cocktail" appetizer.

Today, live oysters can be purchased from the aquarium within the Hua Xing Asian Market on Washtenaw. About a dozen lay in the tank during a recent visit, a tiny remnant of the hundreds of thousands of oysters over the decades that once delighted diners all over Washtenaw County.

Ypsi's Failed Breakfast Cereal

Ypsilanti once had a chance of becoming a Battle Creek–like empire of breakfast cereals.

In 1909, electricity was still making inroads into the city. Only some houses were wired, and the majority were heated with coal. Cars were uncommon. Most women were homemakers, and most men's commute consisted of a walk from home to another part of the city.

Many families got their flour from the Ypsilanti Milling Company on Cross Street near the river. The mill's ad in the March 2, 1909 *Ypsilanti Daily Press* read:

> *The Ypsilanti Mill is now running and turning out a STRICTLY HIGH GRADE FLOUR.*
>
> *Our BLUE LABEL brand is gaining new friends every day. Last week it was just a youngster. This week it is older and you will probably like it better.*
>
> *Further, we want you to try our "TIDAL WAVE" brand. It's a strictly high class patent and worthy of a little assistance from its friends in the way of trial orders. We have on hand BRAN MIDDLINGS, COTTON SEED MEAL, LINSEED MEAL, CALF MEAL…*
>
> *Our wagon is still running* [for home delivery] *and we want you to phone your orders in AT ONCE OR SOONER.*

The hydro-powered mill was an old one, dating from the 1830s. A feature article in the May 23, 1874 *Ypsilanti Commercial* gave an overview of the city businesses of the time. The piece mentions the city mill:

> [The mill stands] *on the east bank of the Huron, above Cross Street bridge. It, or rather the mill of which this is an enlargement, was built in Territorial days* [before Michigan became a state in 1837]. *In 1865 it came into the possession of the Ypsilanti Woolen Mill Company, and by this company was sold to T.C. Owen, Esq., a nephew of E.B. Ward of Detroit, who is also an interested party. The mill is an immense structure. It contains seven run of stone, and at present is turning out 250 barrels of flour per day. It, in addition, grinds 30,000 bushels of grain per year, for the farmers of the vicinity…A side track from the Michigan Central Railroad runs to the door of the mill.*

The side track ran about where Rice Street is today.

Ypsilanti poet-farmer William Lambie raised wheat on his farm just north of town. In his poem "A Harvest Hymn," published in his 1883 book *Life on the Farm*, he lauded the grain:

> *We see the God of nature in bounteous love bestowing,*
> *In every year of life we reap the seed we have been sowing,*
> *Till our barns are filled with plenty and cups are overflowing,*
> *As we are marching on.*
>
> *We have entered on a calling that will never know defeat,*
> *For honor and for daily bread we work in summer's heat,*
> *Ever reaping golden harvests of the finest of the wheat,*
> *When summer days are long.*

The year 1909 was a good one for local wheat production. The Ypsilanti Milling Corporation decided to put some of that wheat into a new venture. It milled it into a breakfast gruel similar to Cream of Wheat.

WHEAT HEARTS

What are they? Well we'll tell you. They are our new breakfast food made from the very best wheat grown; viz, that around Ypsilanti, and ground fresh every day. Why buy breakfast foods made away from home when you can get something here which you know is fresh and which will cost you less money. Ask your grocer for Wheat Hearts.

The Ypsilanti Milling Co.

East Cross St.   Phone 171

Wheat Hearts ads ran only briefly in the local paper. *Author's collection.*

A Different Dining Room

On August 6, 1909, the first ad for "Wheat Hearts" appeared:

WHEAT HEARTS

What are they? Well, we'll tell you. They are our new breakfast food made from the very best wheat grown; viz, that around Ypsilanti, and ground fresh every day. Why buy breakfast foods made away from home when you can get something here which you know is fresh and which will cost you less money. Ask your grocer for Wheat Hearts. The Ypsilanti Milling Co. East Cross St. Phone 171.

The ad ran again on August 10, 12 and 16, as the company waited for Ypsilantians to pester their grocers. Several local grocers ran their own ads during that summer, listing goods and specials. Some listed oatmeal and cornflakes. None listed Ypsilanti Wheat Hearts.

The Ypsilanti Milling Company's ads for Wheat Hearts had vanished by September 1909. Perhaps no one wanted a hot breakfast gruel in August; possibly a fall launch of the cereal might have helped it to succeed. At any rate, Wheat Hearts disappeared. The Ypsilanti Historical Museum holds no packaging artifacts of this forgotten cereal.

Had it caught on, Wheat Hearts might have made Ypsilanti a breakfast cereal empire, renowned from Mackinac to Monroe. Trains could have shipped the cereal to cities around the nation. Citizens could have been humming the catchy Wheat Hearts jingle, perhaps along the lines of:

From the fertile Ypsilanti
To the pantry of my auntie,
Grown and gathered in the summer sun…
It's the gruel you'd be a fool to shun!

Alas, it wasn't to be. Wheat Hearts vanished from the 1909 papers and presumably from local stores—if indeed it had ever been stocked. It hadn't even passed muster to be included with the humble food served in nearby student boardinghouses.

BEAUTIES IN BOARDINGHOUSES

EMU students in 1907 didn't have campus dorms, personal transportation or on-campus meal plans. A humor article in the 1907 *Aurora* yearbook illustrates how different—and in some ways, how timelessly similar—were students' lives.

"A Day at the Normal" (EMU was then known as Normal College) is a chronological account that kicks off in early morning:

> *6 A.M.: Loud ringing of alarm clocks.*
> *6:05 A.M.: Yawns and groans.*
> *6:10 A.M.: General getting up.*
> *6:30 A.M.: Mad scrambling to get to the boarding-house.*
> *6:35 A.M.: Waiting for breakfast.*
> *6:40 A.M.: Waiter appears with a dish of sawdust in one hand and some chopped hay in the other.*

By and large, students rented rooms in family homes throughout the city for living quarters. The school coordinated the placement of students with homeowners willing to house a student or students of either gender—co-ed houses were not allowed (a rule that in later years was relaxed). School

One panel of a student-drawn cartoon in EMU's 1915 *Aurora* yearbook depicted boardinghouse "hash" as an appetizing blend of buttons, safety pins and paper clips. *Author's collection.*

officials kept an eye on the homes in order to make any necessary changes to their "approved homes" list.

A few such private homes also provided meals, but most students subscribed to a meal plan at a separate boardinghouse, whose name derives from the "board," or table. The term "boardinghouse reach" originates from this era, evoking a table full of hungry diners but only one saltshaker. At this time, a week's worth of three daily meals at a boardinghouse cost students about two dollars, or about fifty dollars today.

After leaving their rooming houses and eating breakfast at their boardinghouses, students headed to school:

> *7:00 A.M. Seniors slowly amble towards the Library.*
> *7:50: General evacuation of the Library. Many collisions in the hall. Great crowd of boys at the social corner causes traffic to cease for a time.*
> *7:59: Empty corridors. Re-echoing footsteps in the distance.*
> *8:05: Janitors sit down on the steps for an hour's visit.*
> *8:07:* [Psychology] *Prof. Laird: "I shall keep all these people who are late, after school."*
> *8:10:* [French and German] *Prof. Ford: "How many of you people have had your breakfast this morning?" (Half of the class look silly).*

The Normal was a teacher training school with an on-site grade school where senior Normal students practiced teaching classes under the eye of the dreaded supervising "Critic Teacher."

> *8:50: Seniors rush to the Training School, pleasant (?) anticipation in every feature.*
> *9:05: Critic teacher comes in, notebook in hand.*
> *9:06: Courage flies out of the window.*
> *9:30: Student teacher drops lifeless to the floor.*
> *9:32: She is pushed out of the door to make way for another victim.*

After morning classes came the mad scramble to return to the boardinghouse for lunch, with student couples tending to lag a bit behind. If lunch was eaten expeditiously, there might be time to enjoy another stroll back to school with one's sweetheart.

The EMU yearbook was produced each year by a student group and was initially printed in town. *Author's collection.*

> *11:50: Normal doors are burst open by vast crowds of students. They rush for the boarding houses at break-neck speed.*
> *12: Grub.*
> *12:30 P.M.: Groups of well-filled (?) students issue forth and go down the street in the following order: Miss Ronan and Mr. Engle; Miss Warren and Mr. Miller; Mr. Caswell and a bunch of seven or more; Hugo and Clara; Withenbury and Louise; Roy and Brice; C.P. and Anne; "Doc" and his pockets.*

In the afternoon came class observation time for student teachers, as well as other classes that included music lessons and student teaching feedback critique sessions.

> *12:55 P.M.: The "one o'clock" gong sounds. Groups of light-hearted* [grade school] *children skip towards the Training School, while here and there a solitary senior wends his weary way thither to "observe."*
> *1:30 P.M.: Unearthly screeches from the Conservatory denote the fact that someone is taking a lesson.*

3 P.M.: Critic Meeting. Every one hustles to get there and learn how to receive the worst "slams" with a smiling countenance.

In the afternoon, sports practices began, occasionally interrupted by the diversion of a wondrous contraption then rare in the city.

4 P.M.: The Tennis Courts are full of people bobbing around picking up white balls. The baseball boys trot around after [Coach] Schulte.
4:15 P.M.: An automobile goes down Cross Street. All occupation ceases.
4:20 P.M.: Occupations are again resumed.
5:15 P.M.: The studious people in the Library are requested to bring books to the desk and get reserved books.

The school day was over. Students could return to their boardinghouse for dinner.

5:30 P.M.: "Hash time" has arrived. The odors issuing forth from the doors and windows proclaim the ingredients.

Those ingredients were lambasted in a satirical "Menu from a Leading Boarding House" article, published in the 1918 *Aurora*'s jokes section:

BREAKFAST: *Corn Flakes, Toasted*
Diluted Fluid of Bovine
Encrusted Doughpiles,
Browned Meat, in absentia
Essence of H2O, Filtered
Mock Coffee, with condemned milk
Napkins

DINNER [today called lunch]: *Soup in bowls*
Bread, individual slices
Vegetables sometimes
Roast Beef a la tuffo
Essence H2O refiltered
Mock Coffee heated
Pie Filet de Vacuum
Napkins, Folded

The *Aurora* cartoon tweaked dandyish Ann Arbor boys who visited the campus, the trials of student teachers and tentative romantic pursuits. *Author's collection.*

SUPPER [dinner]: *Beef, resurrected*
Potatoes, with eyes
Hot Canines, deanimated
Aqua pura, in glasses
Mock Coffee again
Dried apricots, bonded vintage 1763
Cookies, a la hardtack from Plymouth
Napkins, Refolded

After dinner, the students' evenings were free for study...or less scholastic pursuits.

6 P.M.: Pear [a joke on "pair," or couple] *time again.*
6:30 P.M.: The beauties of the Huron are viewed by twilight.

Visiting another rooming house was allowed but supervised. All too soon, the rooming houses' citywide and ironclad curfew of 10:00 p.m. would arrive, and visitors had to leave their charming companions. Tomorrow was another school day.

10 P.M.: Many doors are opened and young men come out.
1 P.M.: The streets are quiet. The High School clock and the moon keep a silent watch over the slumbering town.

Part II

OUT OF THE KITCHEN

THE ACCIDENTAL PHOTOGRAPHER

The sitting woman smoothed a tiny wrinkle in her lap. She glanced up at the large skylight partially screened with gauzy curtains. It was a May day in 1872. Large fluffy clouds sailed silently beyond the glass. The photographer was taking a while adjusting something on the camera. Finally it was ready. "Look at me, please," said the photographer. *Click.*

"That was very good, thank you," said Mary Parsons, Ypsilanti's only nineteenth-century female studio photographer.

Born in Vermont in January 1838, Mary Elizabeth married John Harrison Parsons when she was twenty-one and he twenty-five. The couple followed other westernbound migrants, and during the Civil War both taught in Ohio. By war's end the couple had two sons, Dayton W. and Frank John.

The conflict had decimated the student-aged population of young men. In 1865, John and Mary came north to Ypsilanti. John bought the equipment of retiring photographer J.A. Crane and created his own studio. It occupied part of the top floor of Ypsilanti's post office building, then located on the west side of North Huron next to Pearl Street. It was a good location near the bustling downtown on Michigan Avenue. Mary helped run the business and kept house in the family's apartment, next to the studio.

Five years into the work, the couple were supporting a family of six that included nine-year-old Dayton, five-year-old Frank, three-year-old Viola and the baby, Ina. Mary was also pregnant with another child. After New Year's Day 1871, she gave birth to a son, naming him John Jr.

A portrait of Mary from circa 1880, photographer unknown. *Courtesy of Ypsilanti Archives.*

The baby's namesake was deathly ill. John was diagnosed with consumption, or tuberculosis, Washtenaw County's leading cause of death in the late nineteenth century. The disease accounted for 15 percent of all county deaths.

After a struggle, John died on February 24. On May 13, John Jr. also died of consumption. Mary did not have relatives in the area. She had to forge ahead or see her remaining children suffer. She became a professional photographer.

"For the benefit of any sister seeking a place among the limited situations for our sex, I would say that women can succeed in any department of the photograph business," Mary wrote in a letter to well-known journalist Martha Louise Rayne, who published it in her bestselling 1884 book *What Can a Woman Do: Or, Her Position in the Business and Literary World*:

> *I should not have chosen it as a life-work had not circumstances pressed me into service. My husband and myself were both teachers when we were married. He was a teacher of a commercial school when the war broke out and took so many of the class of young men that were beginning a business education that he dropped his professorship and took up photography. I*

learned printing of him, and afterwards, as his health failed, I assisted in different departments, and when he finally died, leaving me with a family of five little ones, I took his advice, and have carried on the work successfully enough to support my family ever since.

...I hope you will make it a successful medium in giving encouragement to our sex, compelled by adverse circumstances to support themselves, for all cannot be teachers, clerks, or seamstresses.

The 1873 Scripps, Clark and Polk's *Michigan State Gazetteer and Business Directory* lists 195 Ypsilanti business concerns and businesspeople. Only ten businesswomen are listed. Mrs. Baker and Mrs. Case were milliners (hat makers) on Cross Street, Mrs. Curtis and Mrs. Shrieves were milliners on Huron, Mrs. Earing was a milliner in the Hewitt block and Mrs. Martin was a milliner on Michigan Avenue. Miss Coe was a milliner on Huron and Miss Rogers was a milliner on Michigan Avenue. Miss Cramer was an agent of the Howe sewing machine company, whose office was on Michigan Avenue. Miss Casey was a manufacturer of "rats," the colloquial term for women's hairpieces.

The information is at least two years out of date: John Parsons is included in the listing as a photographer, when by that time Mary was operating the shop. She did it well and ran an ad in the June 13, 1874 *Ypsilanti Commercial*: "PHOTOGRAPH GALLERY. Mrs. Parsons has been making improvements in the sky-light of her gallery, giving much quicker time in the taking of negatives and

The reverse of one of Mary's 1870s-era cartes-de-visites shows her studio logo. *Courtesy of Ypsilanti Archives.*

a nice effect for 'shadow pictures.' She is trying to keep up with the times in all that will help to improve the art. Those wishing a good picture give her a call."

Mary produced cartes-de-visites and cabinet cards. Cartes-de-visites were portraits about the size of an elongated baseball card and were a very popular keepsake to trade with friends and relatives. One of the cartes-de-visites Mary made bears her colophon on the reverse, in the elaborate style of the day. Cabinet cards were photographs whose larger size of $4\frac{1}{4}$ by $6\frac{1}{2}$ inches soon made them more popular than the older cartes-de-visites. Both techniques used albumen prints mounted on stiff board.

By the time Charles Chapman published his *History of Washtenaw County* in 1881, Mary merited a mention. "Since the death of her husband, Mrs. Parsons has carried on the photograph business. The work in the operating-room is done by an assistant, but the finishing and printing she does herself. Her business has increased and been generally successful."

A dozen years into her work, Mary received a marriage proposal from Erastus Samson, a fellow native Vermonter and the owner of Ypsilanti's first drugstore, where he also sold whiskey, gin and some dry goods. Erastus had lost his wife, Georgianne, in 1882. On March 30, 1883, Mary and Erastus married. She was forty-five and he was sixty-one. Mary moved into the Samson home at 302 Cross Street.

Mary sold her studio and all the equipment that she and her husband had accumulated since the business's beginning almost twenty years ago. Her career as a photographer was over. She settled into a comfortable life.

Erastus and Mary remained married for twenty-two years until his death at age eighty-three in 1905. Mary lived to age eighty and died in 1918. Her photographic legacy is housed in various family albums in the Ypsilanti Archives.

The Male Suffragette

"Baby suffrage" is what one Detroit newspaper snidely proposed in 1874. In that year, Michigan voted on whether to remove the word "male" from a part of its constitution related to voting. The paper sneered that infants voting in polling booths would be the next step if women were given the vote.

Newspapers of the era often served as explicit vehicles for their editors' opinions and prejudices. As they did with the temperance issue, papers across Michigan chose sides in the suffrage question in its key year of 1874. Their prosuffrage and antisuffrage positions reflected the divided opinions not just on the national level, but, as in Ypsilanti, even on a municipal level.

Edited by Charles Woodruff, the *Ypsilanti Sentinel* was against suffrage for women. It regularly published editorials that disparaged the idea and criticized the *Sentinel's* competing paper, the *Ypsilanti Commercial*, which was led by arguably the most outspoken editor in Ypsilanti history.

Charles Rich Pattison was born in New York in 1824. His father, Samuel Warren Pattison, and mother, Phebe Atwood Pattison, brought him to Michigan Territory when he was twelve years old. According to Charles Chapman's 1881 *History of Washtenaw County*, "[F]rom 1836 to 1840, he devoted his time to fishing and hunting and clerking in a store."

Pattison was educated at home and by age seventeen was teaching in a nearby school. After more work as an educator and school principal, Pattison became a University of Michigan student at age twenty-two. He was a member of the literary society Alpha Nu and for three years edited the literary journal *Sibyl*.

After graduation, Charles studied at Newton Theological Seminary in Massachusetts. He graduated in 1853 and served as pastor in Baptist churches in Pontiac and Grass Lake. He married Ellen Frey in 1854.

On January 1, 1864, at age forty, Pattison bought the office and printing equipment of an Ypsilanti paper called the *Herald*. He began publishing the *True Democrat*, later renamed the *Commercial*.

The *Commercial* reflected the Baptist pastor turned editor's pro-temperance, prosuffrage opinions. The paper succeeded, and Charles moved into a larger printing house at the southeast corner of Cross and Huron Streets.

At times, the office seemed more like a fortification and Pattison less an editor than a large piece of artillery firing blasts at saloonkeepers, advocates of standard time and his archnemesis, editor Woodruff at the *Sentinel*.

"The most absurd charge ever trumped up," said Pattison in the May 30, 1874 *Commercial*, "is that 'Free Love' so called has anything to do with woman suffrage. No man, unless innately depraved, would make such a base charge."

Pattison continued: "Says the *Sentinel*, 'Is not [free love advocate] Victoria Woodhull in favor of woman's suffrage?' No doubt of it. It is the only subject in regard to which she seems to indicate any soundness of mind." Pattison wound up his editorial with one last blast at Woodruff: "His real trouble is that if the women vote they will smash his darling idols, the saloons."

Pattison attacked the *Sentinel* again on June 20, 1874, for allegedly misrepresenting the *Woman's Journal* a prosuffrage publication:

> *Our contemporary exhibits his general misanthropy by misquoting* [and] *distorting sentences in the* Women's Journal. *He knows, for he is not altogether inane, notwithstanding his knavish propensities, that the entire tenor of the* Woman's Journal *is in favor of the highest cultivation of domestic and marital ties, the ennobling of these rather than their abolition.*
>
> *The* Sentinel *has an amazing affinity for Victoria Woodhull. It can't let the poor woman alone. If a copy of her paper can be found it turns up in the* Sentinel *office. The advocates of woman suffrage in Michigan don't affiliate in that direction and don't keep track of such journals. The* Sentinel *naturally gravitates to carrion as a starving man does to food.*

When suffrage leader Elizabeth Cady Stanton took an 1874 tour of Michigan, she spoke in Jackson Prison, Ypsilanti, Detroit and other spots. "The *Detroit Post* is in tantrums about Mrs. Stanton's canvass of the State," Pattison said in the June 6 *Commercial*. "It copies every miserable slimy slander in regard to her speeches. Mrs. Stanton's speech in [Ypsilanti] was entirely unexceptionable. It was mild, persuasive, eloquent, argumentative, and convincing…Common sensed men will reason that a cause that can only be met by innuendo and misrepresentation must be based on the rock and worthy their confidence."

Pattison was not the only prosuffrage man in town. Another was Professor Estabrook, the head of Normal College and a regent of UM. "[His stance on suffrage] has significance as he is one of the leading educators in the State," said Pattison in the July 11 *Commercial*. Many local clergymen also supported the cause, according to Pattison. "A large proportion of our ministry, especially in the Methodist and Baptist churches, are in favor of woman's suffrage," he said in the May 9 *Commercial*.

Pattison wrote a letter to the governor of the Wyoming Territory. The territory had given women the vote in 1869, the first state or territory to permanently do so. He printed the governor's reply in the July 11 *Commercial*:

Dear Sir.

In regard to your enquiries as to the success of woman suffrage in this Territory, its influence upon the women, the men, whether good or bad, its effect upon the body politic, I would respond affirmatively in every way. I send you a copy of my message of last November as an expression of my views. Michigan, rich in every element—material, intellectual, and moral—that goes to make up a State, with her famous University and no less famous Common School system needs this beneficent reform superadded, to constitute her a truly republican commonwealth and the model State of the Union. Wyoming has taken the lead of the Territories in adopting this reform. We trust that Michigan will pioneer her sister States.

Yours very truly,
J.A. Campbell.

The 1874 Michigan vote for the suffrage amendment was defeated, 135,957 to 40,077. It wouldn't be until 1918 that Michigan male voters voted to approve women's suffrage. Pattison did not live to see that vote—he died in Florida in 1908. But it's likely that his efforts, in his day, played a small part in helping to eventually bring about equal voting rights for women.

THO' LOVE BE COLD, DO NOT DESPAIR

An imagined scene at the 1893 World's Columbian Exposition: The whispery swish of a strolling fairgoer's dress falls silent in front of a woman's clothing display. Tastefully arranged near the scarves from New York's Altman Summer Neckwear Company and the wares of Chicago's Ivorine Collar and Cuff Company are both cream and white union suits. Amid the babble of voices and the smell of popcorn in the vast hall, the woman studies the finely knit undergarments. She reaches out and touches one made of silk, another of wool and a third made of cotton. The nationally known union suits were the proud product of a Michigan mill located in the small community of Ypsilanti.

Perched on a bank of the Huron River at Forest Avenue, the six-story Hay & Todd woolen mill, like many nineteenth-century Ypsilanti businesses, was powered by water. The current moved swiftly there, just downstream from a bend, in a river that ran about five feet higher than today.

From the time the community was first settled, the site had been a popular commercial venue. In 1828, a flour mill and sawmill were built there by David Hardy and Asa Reading. In 1839, they were joined by another flour mill, this one built by Arden Ballard. Twelve years later, the Hardy & Reading mill was torn down. And in October 1856, the Ballard Eagle mill met its own fate when it was consumed in a fire.

But the Eagle mill site was too important to leave lying in ruins. In the 1860s, several of the city's wealthiest businessmen gathered to make plans for its use. Despite the state's profitable wheat crop, Daniel Quirk, Cornelius Cornwell, Isaac Conklin and Robert Hemphill had a different idea.

Wool Manufacturing Comes to Ypsilanti

Between 1840 and 1860, Michigan's population of sheep increased from 100,000 to more than ten times that number. During that time, wool output jumped from 153,375 pounds to nearly 4 million pounds and leapt again to 11 million pounds in 1880. In 1865, Michigan provided one-tenth of the nation's wool crop, almost all of it produced in the southern section of the Lower Peninsula. Washtenaw County was the top producer that year, with a wool harvest, or "clip," of 1.25 million pounds—most of it from Spanish merino sheep.

The award-winning Vermont-born merino "Premier" belonged to Ypsilanti sheep farmer J. Evarts Smith. *Author's collection.*

As a mostly agrarian state, Michigan lacked the capital to build factories to work the wool, forcing sheep farmers to ship their supply out of state for processing. In an appeal to the Michigan Senate for a tax break for woolen processors, Cornwell stated, "The extension of this important manufacture is of great interest to the State, the climate rendering woolen clothing necessary the greater portion of the year, and because it furnishes the producer a ready home market." These circumstances persuaded Cornwell, Quirk and their co-investors to establish a woolen mill in 1865.

Just three years later, wool prices began dropping in the market's anticipation, ultimately mistaken, of the revival of the South's post–Civil War cotton crop. Shortly after, sheep farmers in Michigan and across the Midwest began culling or slaughtering their herds.

The original investors then sold the mill to William Hay and Frank Todd. While the two men were at the helm, the wool market revived and the factory's glory days began.

Impact of the Dress Reform Movement

At first, the Hay & Todd mill manufactured fine yarns, knitted hose, leggings, hats and "nubias" (lightweight knitted head scarves). In about 1885, however, the company made a risky decision in response to a controversial social movement, one addressed at the 1893 World's Columbian Exposition.

Northwest of the Manufactures and Liberal Arts Building, where the mill had displayed its union suits, stood the Women's Building. Ann Jenness Miller, known as "the apostle of dress reform," spoke there on the subject of "Dress Improvement" during the exposition's Congress of Women.

"One who carefully examines the pages of fashion magazines," she said, "and looks into the history of dress, will find…that there has never been any attempt upon the part of fashion makers to clothe the body consistently… The body has been cramped and distorted, its requirements for health and comfort disregarded according to the caprice of fashion's arbiters… The fundamental laws of beauty have been violated, and the human form robbed of its expression to what end? Who can answer?"

Popularized in 1851 when Amelia Bloomer first wore her eponymous clothes, the dress reform movement sought to free women from overly restrictive clothing. Given the discomfort of Victorian-era undergarments

The western side of the factory in 1916, looking toward the Huron River. The structure at right is the factory's bicycle garage. *Courtesy of Ypsilanti Archives.*

and their invisibility to the public eye, underwear reform seemed like a promising starting point. Jenness, Bloomer, Bloomer's friend Elizabeth Cady Stanton and Battle Creek's John Harvey Kellogg were among those who advocated for the movement.

Jenness strongly approved of Ypsilanti underwear: "It gives me great pleasure to state that women who are wearing Ypsilanti union suits are enthusiastic in its praise. This is necessarily so, for the garment is perfect, and I am sanguine that the day is not far distant when this form of union garment will have taken the place of all others."

The Mill Begins to Advertise

Although she had a Washington, D.C., address, Jenness's knowledge of the small Michigan city's union suits wasn't an anomaly. Advertisements for the goods had spread from local to national publications by 1891. An ad from that year in *Harper's* magazine touted "Ypsilanti Dress Reform Underwear," as did promotions in *Lippincott's Magazine*, the *Cosmopolitan*, the *Chautauquan*, the *Century* and *Life*.

The ads popularized company slogans, such as "Tho' love be cold, do not despair—There's Ypsilanti Underwear." "Never Rip—Never Tear—Ypsilanti Underwear," noted another. Among the claims the manufacturers made was that "Ypsilanti Underwear is the Standard Underwear of Civilization" and "the only sanitary underwear, and endorsed by the leading medical professionals."

The promotions paid off in spades. In a travelogue titled *Abroad at Home: American Ramblings, Observations, and Adventures of Julian Street*, published in New York shortly after the turn of the century, Street observed:

> *On the railroad journey between Detroit and Battle Creek we passed two towns which have attained a fame entirely disproportionate to their size: Ann Arbor, with about fifteen thousand inhabitants, celebrated as a seat of learning; and Ypsilanti, with about six thousand, celebrated as, so to speak, a seat of underwear.*
>
> *One expects an important college town to be well known, but a manufacturing town with but six thousand inhabitants must have done something in particular to have acquired [a] national reputation. In the case of Ypsilanti it has been done by magazine advertising—the advertising of [its] underwear.*

"Ypsilantis" Enter Popular Culture

Hay & Todd undergarments were sold in dry goods stores from Baltimore to Los Angeles and from Toronto to Dallas. The firm added Detroit and Ann Arbor branch factories. The garments were so well known that the name "Ypsilantis" became a generic term for long underwear. A limerick published in Stanton Vaughn's 1904 anthology *Limerick Lyrics* celebrated the clothing:

> *A sculptor of nymphs and Bacchantes*
> *Omitted the coaties and panties.*
> *But a kind-hearted Madam,*
> *Who knew where they had 'em,*
> *Donated some warm "Ypsilanties."*

In reviewing Ypsilanti mineral bath advertisements for the January 1898 issue of the New York–based trade magazine *Printer's Ink: A Journal for Advertisers*, Charles Bates wrote, "There is one thing about the word Ypsilanti, and that is, it is so indelibly connected with Ypsilanti underwear, that in first looking at these advertisements before me, it struck me that I had received a batch of advertisements intended to state that Ypsilanti underwear was good to be worn by persons troubled with rheumatism, blood and skin diseases."

The February 1900 issue of *Good Housekeeping* magazine featured an anagram game whose theme was "Bits of Wearing Apparel." The answer to the clue "Try a new rude sail-pin" was "Ypsilanti underwear."

One factor that advanced the clothing's notoriety was the use of female models in its advertisements. In the October 1898 issue of the *Philistine* magazine, an anonymous writer identified only by the Latin name for the Greek god of medicine, Aesculapius, vented his spleen: "Some time ago it became necessary for me to enter a protest in these pages on the subject of Art and Underwear." He then drew a parallel to the popular contemporaneous union suit manufacturer Jaeger. "The Ypsilanti Yagerites [*sic*] with unblushing foreheads, encouraged by the High Class Monthlies, carried matters so far that as a man of family, with growing sons and daughters, I could no longer admit the Family *Press* to my home. Fortunately I succeeded in checking the exhibition without calling in the aid of [anti-vice crusader Anthony] Comstock."

The Infamous Ypsilanti Mural

At the height of its success, the Ypsilanti underwear factory also sported a fifteen-foot-high mural of a curvaceous woman clad only in a union suit, clearly visible to train riders passing by. Local lore says that some travelers averted their gaze because they objected to the image's sexuality, while others made sure to look in order to be properly scandalized.

In addition to inciting ire, becoming a household name and starring in the women's dress reform movement, the Hay & Todd mill—renamed the Ypsilanti Underwear Company about 1905—employed more women than any other city business of its time. Some even rose to management positions.

Many women rode to the factory on another agent of female emancipation, the bicycle. They parked them in the factory's "bicycle house" just southeast of the mill building. In just a few years, however, the factory, bicycle house and accompanying outbuildings would all be gone.

The Business Declines

As the dress reform movement fell out of favor around the turn of the century, the underwear company adjusted its advertising strategy accordingly. Late 1890s and early 1900s ads in the *Century*, *Frank Leslie's Popular Monthly* and other publications dropped the descriptor "Dress Reform Underwear" in favor of the phrase "Health Underwear." But the tide had already turned.

Shortly after the turn of the century, the Ypsilanti Underwear Company began to face financial difficulties. One reason, it's alleged, is that the steady spread of central heating in homes made the garments obsolete. In 1906, the company closed its Ann Arbor branch. Soon after, its Detroit branch followed.

In spring 1907, the Ypsilanti factory's mortgage holder, the Union Trust Company, began foreclosure proceedings. The factory was subsequently closed and then purchased by the Syracuse-based Oak Knitting Company. This action proved unprofitable to the New York concern, and the building was resold and then leased by the Ray Battery Company for a few years. Finally, it stood empty. In 1933, all of the buildings were demolished.

But the mill was not forgotten. "As it was an old building with some walls cracked and unsafe it was considered a fire trap and was condemned by the state fire marshal as a fire hazard," noted former underwear company worker Sara Schaff in a factory history she read before a gathering of former workers that August. "[The marshal] deemed it wise to have it torn down… while doing so they came across some floors and walls of the old flour mills in the north east corner of the basement."

The workers Schaff addressed that day in Ypsilanti's Prospect Park were enjoying their annual company reunion. The mostly female members of what could be called the "Underwear Club" continued to meet in the park for a potluck, ice cream and fond reminiscing until 1941.

Today, the mill site is occupied by the Ypsilanti branch of the vintage auto restoration firm RM Classic Cars. A few large boulders in the river under the Forest Avenue bridge may be remnants of the mill dam. But a lone example of the garments that once occupied dresser drawers in homes across the nation hangs on display in the Ypsilanti Historical Museum. That petite, dainty women's suit of underwear serves as testament to the city's onetime preeminence as the home of the "Standard Underwear of Civilization."

CORSET WARRIORS

In 2010, census canvassers went door to door, asking their ten questions about each home's residents, their individual sex, race and age, as well as whether the property was mortgaged. Imagine if they'd asked each woman about her underwear preferences.

Thirteen thousand women were asked that very question in 1892 by Michigan state officials. The officials were male, but oddly enough it was women who were responsible for inserting the undergarment question into the state-funded survey.

The winding road to this naughty quiz began with an 1880s state governor who was concerned about the working class. In his 1883 inaugural address, Michigan governor Josiah Begole proposed the creation of a state bureau to collect information about labor conditions. "Paupers and criminals," he said, "the fish that swim in our rivers and lakes, and the cattle that graze in our fields, are cared for by commissioners appointed by the State. A large class of our citizens…have no one whose especial duty it is to investigate their condition…I refer to the laboring class."

Begole had reason for concern. The following year's report by the new Bureau of Labor and Industrial Statistics summarized data from fourteen major manufacturing cities. It was found that the average workday was ten hours long. Sawmill, salt mill and shingle mill employees worked eleven to fifteen hours per day and streetcar drivers up to seventeen.

Worker accommodations at many job sites were deplorable. The 1884 report mentioned

> *the appalling poverty and squalidity of the poor* [Wayne County] *brickyard laborers. The destitution and wretchedness of life is rendered much more apparent…by reason of the filthy, dilapidated, little hovels into which the laborer is crowded. These usually consist of one room and a shed, and are built of ten-foot boards, standing on end, with the floor raised about two feet, making a room about eight feet high, by about ten feet square.*

The average family, said the report, consisted of six people living in those one hundred square feet.

The not unsympathetic report continued: "Unorganized, untaught, uncared for, seemingly unambitious, [immigrant] strangers in a strange land, with every waking hour devoted to satisfying the needs and desires of the physical man, these people seem scarcely to realize their humanity."

The 1884 report took a cursory look at women in the workplace. It noted the daily wages of 502 women across the state. The average was $0.74 ($18.00 today), compared to $1.77 for men ($42.00 today). The three women's professions whose wage range offered a chance to earn up to $2.00 per day included clerks, dressmakers and laundresses. The report also examined the wages of 500 domestics, or house servants. Most domestics earned between $2.00 and $3.50 per day (their pay included a stipend for personal expenses), but if living at their employer's home, they were on call around the clock.

Despite low wages and a limited variety of "appropriate" jobs on the distaff side, women entered the workforce in ever greater numbers. In 1892, the state's nine-year-old Bureau of Labor decided to focus on this growing trend and devoted most of the yearly report to an analysis of women's work.

Among the bureau agents' survey questions were two that had been included at the request of progressive women's societies concerned about working women's welfare. In the working world, the well-meaning questions proved offensive. "A great many of whom the questions were asked thought no one had any right to receive any answer to them, not comprehending the statistical purposes in view," groused the report's writer.

One question asked which church the women attended (with the assumption that they were Christian) and whether they belonged to a ladies' or community society. It seems probable that the forward-thinking women who'd campaigned to include this question viewed church and society membership as marks of a wholesome spiritual and moral condition.

The other question—pity the poor male bureau official asking this of hundreds of female strangers—inquired whether the lady wore a corset:

This question was requested to be asked of the women wage-workers by ladies interested in the welfare of their sex with a desire of ascertaining, if possible, the effect of the wearing of corsets upon women workers, and also to get an expression from the women themselves as to their effect upon health.

An interesting feature of this report [is that] comparing the health of those who report not wearing corsets with the health of those [that] do, the percentage of good health we find largely in favor of those who report no.

Taken in the context of the era's dress reform movement, and a growing women's rights movement in general, the question is less intrusive than radical. Progressive women sought greater freedom for their sex, and a safe place to begin reform was where it couldn't be seen and jeered—namely, among the nineteenth century's complicated and restrictive undergarments, hidden under outerwear.

Many working-class women agreed with dress reform. "I know from extensive observation that the wearing of corsets is very injurious to the health of women," said one female worker quoted in the bureau's survey. "[I] have been deeply interested in the ideas as promulgated by the Chautauqua dress reform ladies which this year [have] attracted more popular attention than ever before…the principal motive [of the movement is] to give greater freedom of motion to women, to dispense with the health-breaking corset, and to shift the weight of clothing from the waist…to the shoulders, where it ought to be. It is a serious matter, this dress reform idea."

"I advise no one to wear them. I think them injurious to working people," said another working woman survey respondent. "In winter," said another. "Sometimes when not working," said one. Echoing the sentiments of many, however, one woman snapped, "It is a personal affair."

Of the 13,000 women surveyed, about 3,400 said that they wore corsets; 232 said they didn't. Nearly 10,000 did not respond. (No figures on the number who slapped the questioner's face.) After completing and turning in the report, bureau officials likely felt relief to be free of the troublesome, embarrassing work and the indignant women.

But one final feminine sally blasted forth from the December 1892 issue of the *Journal of the American Statistical Association*. Statistician Laura Salmon had pored over the bureau's report. "It is a matter of no small moment," she began approvingly, "to stimulate among working women themselves a discussion concerning the sanitary conditions under which they work, the unhygienic features of women's dress, the possibility of saving wages."

Salmon, however, took a dim view of the published report. After criticizing the bureau's ramshackle methodology, she excoriated its mangling of English. Valuable information, she said, should be presented in a readable form for the public. "[I]nasmuch as the general public has yet to be educated to consider statistical reports interesting and valuable reading," she said, "the presentation of statistical material in…[an] interesting manner is scarcely second in importance to [facts]."

"The majority of readers whose interest in statistics has yet to be won," she continued—perhaps with exasperation at the statistics-oblivious public—"are repelled by...'data' used uniformly as a singular noun, the not infrequent use of a plural subject with a singular verb and the reverse, [the antique term] 'widow lady,'...and a score of inaccurate expressions too long to quote."

"But far worse than this slovenly use of English—bad as it is," she persisted, building up a good head of steam, "is its undignified use. 'Grass widow,' 'gents,' 'a hustling city,' savor of the street corner rather than suggest the highest industrial authority in a great commonwealth."

In closing, Laura blew the whistle: "Accuracy of mathematical work and grasp of statistical principles ought not to be incompatible with the presentation of a subject, if not in elegant, at least not in slovenly English."

The gavel had fallen. From that day to this, the State of Michigan has never again dared to question women about their undies.

FACTORY GIRLS OF 1910

Their work was dirty, dangerous and underpaid. They worked next to men but earned half men's pay. Predating Rosie the Riveter, these forgotten local women had no less grit.

In 1910, 25 percent of women nationwide worked outside the home. Ypsilanti women held a wide variety of jobs around town. Julia King held a prestigious post as a professor of civics and history at the Michigan State Normal College, now EMU. Sarah Arnot worked as an assistant at the school.

Margaret and Martha Allardyce ran their "Allardyce Sisters" dressmaking shop at 207 North Washington, one block west of the Ypsilanti Historical Museum. The widow Libbie Beal headed a boardinghouse at 412 Brower (now College Place). Florence Allmendinger worked as a dental assistant for Herbert Harper in the Hewitt block (whose ground floor now houses Mix boutique). Maude Carpenter was in charge of general delivery at the post office.

But seventy-eight women in twenty-eight of the largest factories in town held positions far removed from the quiet classroom or tidy dental office. Their work in noisy places cluttered with machinery was exhausting, sometimes hazardous and poorly paid. Their standard shift was ten hours per day, beginning at 7:00 a.m. and ending at 6:00 p.m., with an hour off for lunch. They operated machines that often lacked safety guards, in an era long before OSHA. One false move sometime in those ten hours could result in a scalping, a crushed arm or worse.

Yet they worked on, earning money for their families, producing a wide range of goods and ignoring those who sneered that they were socially inferior, even vulgar. They were Ypsilanti's factory girls.

In 1910, Ypsilanti's former leading employer of women, the underwear factory on Forest Avenue at the river, had recently closed after a more than forty-year run. In its late nineteenth-century heyday, the factory had employed 250 women. No 1910 factory had that many. The town's top five employers of women collectively gave jobs to only 71 female workers, despite the fact that women's labor was a bargain compared to men's.

The Horner Specialty Shoe Company at 17–21 Cross Street in Depot Town employed four women. Among them was twenty-one-year-old Neva Thayer, who worked as a shoe designer and craftswoman. Neva boarded with her parents, William and Christie, at the nearby family home at 417 Oak. Many factory girls lived with their parents—seen as more respectable than living alone—often handing over a portion of their earnings.

Ruth McNeal worked at the shoe factory as a forelady, supervising the stitching of the company's athletic shoes and "Indian shoes," or casual moccasin-style shoes used during camping or for slippers at home.

Across town at 301 Michigan Avenue, the *Ypsi Press* also employed four women. Nella Nowell kept the *Press*'s books. Elizabeth O'Brien worked at the paper as a press feeder, someone who inks the roller or platen of a printing press and feeds in paper to be printed. Grace Maddux also worked as a press feeder alongside her brother, printing press operator Ernest. After work, the two went home together to the family home at 28 East Michigan Avenue that the siblings shared with their parents, Charles and Elizabeth.

The White Steam Laundry Company at 28 North Huron employed thirteen women. Nellie McDade laundered and wrung the heavy, dripping batches of clothes. Edith Jackson and Catherine Donahue ironed Nellie's freshly wrung items. May Lyon worked as a sorter, and Clara Schmid kept track of finances.

The town's second-largest employer of women in 1910 was the forty-three-year-old Peninsular Paper Mill. Seventeen women worked in various jobs around the plant, tending to different sections of the immense machinery that churned pulp slurry into finished paper. In addition to the

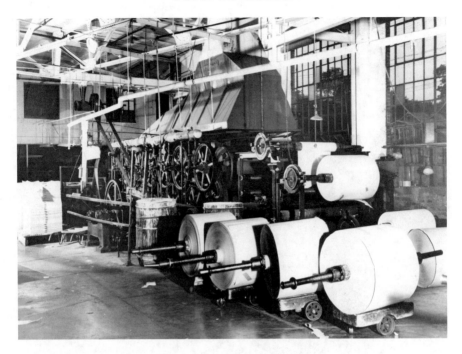

Paper rolls ready for delivery. *Courtesy of Ypsilanti Archives.*

female machine operators, Alta Shaw kept the books. The Peninsular mill was known to be one of the better places for women to work. Their pay wasn't docked for mistakes, as it was at the dress stay manufactory across town and as it had been at the underwear factory.

The city's leading employer of women in 1910 was the Scharf Tag, Label and Box Company at 111–117 Pearl Street (now Congdon's Hardware). Thirty-three women worked to produce the company's catalogues, boxes, printed engravings, labels, job printing projects, *Aurora* yearbooks from the Normal College and tags—lots of tags. At least eight women at Scharf were tag makers: Ina King, Charlotte Matevie, Mattie Misener, Flora Williams, sisters Edith and Marie Ross, Laura Sieber and Katherine Spencer.

Scharf's large and noisy factory floor held numerous specialized printing and cutting machines. Operating them were Katherine Fay, Anna Kircher, May Peters and Grace Randall. Printing presses also occupied the space. *Press* feeders included Mathilda and Ruth Richards. Mildred Schlicht worked as a stenographer. Caroline Fruenter and sisters Anastasia and Johanna Panek

Left: The 1901 Scharf logo's heraldic splendor. *Author's collection.*

Below: The 1907 Scharf logo displayed some of the company's products. *Author's collection.*

were box makers. Bessie Moore and Ida Twist worked as folders. Ethel Glanfield was a bill clerk. Barbara Disbrow served as forewoman.

Today, all of the factories are gone, though the buildings, with the exception of the paper mill, remain. Whether stacking card stock in the tag machine, feeding a press, making paper or designing shoes, Ypsilanti's unsung factory girls created useful products and added to the hum of industry in 1910 Ypsilanti.

YPSILANTI'S WALDORF-ASTORIA

Eula Beardsley and Gladys Huston exited the front door of their Ypsilanti rooming house at Adams and Pearl one late December day in 1924.

"Colder than I thought," said Gladys. Eula pulled shut the front door. "You'll warm up at that big lunch today." The pair walked one block east on Pearl Street, passing rows of shiny black cars at the Wiedman auto dealership to their left. They crossed Washington, heading toward the door of the elegant new Huron Hotel on the northeast corner of Pearl and Washington.

A vintage postcard shows the entrance off Pearl Street. *Courtesy of Ypsilanti Archives.*

Two years earlier, the only accommodations the city could offer guests were at the old-fashioned Hawkins House on Michigan Avenue between Washington and Adams. Built in the nineteenth century, the place had a worn-out and rustic atmosphere. The Ypsilanti Board of Commerce decided that the city needed a modern, attractive hotel. It sold shares of stock to city residents, raised $200,000 and built the hotel in eight months, adding two additional floors two years later.

With a restaurant on the first floor, a "sample room" in which gentlemen could select cigars and tidy, comfortable rooms upstairs, the hotel soon became the hub of downtown activity. Downtown workers met there for lunch, organizations booked the restaurant for banquets and awards ceremonies and traveling businessmen kept the rooms full.

"Good morning, ladies," said the doorman, dressed neatly in a military-style uniform. Forty-nine-year-old Howard Henson was one of the hotel's two porters. He hauled luggage into and out of the hotel and ran occasional errands for guests. It was a demanding job but was considered a good one for a black man in 1920s Ypsilanti. Howard supported his wife, Roxanna, and his sons, Walter and Howard. Roxanna could afford to stay at home with the boys, who eventually got a little sister, Martha. In a few years, Howard would buy his own home.

Eula and Gladys entered the empty coffee shop on the west side of the building, passing the front desk. The clerk, twenty-seven-year-old Fay Zongker, looked up and gave them a wave. They walked past the shining black tables surrounded by walls painted black on their bottom third and then gold, up to a black frieze near the ceiling.

A savory scent of ham came from the kitchen on the north side of the hotel. The two women went into the kitchen and greeted their fellow waitresses: Alice Lyons, Gladys Douglas and Flora Snyder. All of the hotel's five waitresses were scheduled today to handle the expected holiday shopper crowd for the $1.25 lunch ($15.00 in today's money). Three cooks busied themselves in back.

The women looked over the menu. Today's appetizers were hearts of celery and queen olives, followed by a light consommé. Then diners could choose baked halibut, fried chicken, ham, steak or prime rib for an entrée, which came with salad, wax beans, rolls and mashed potatoes or candied yams. Desserts included pie, ice cream or nesselrode pudding, a frozen chestnut custard with nuts and dried cherries.

Out of the Kitchen

A woman in a white apron came in the other end of the kitchen and greeted the waitresses. Emma Sparrow poured herself a cup of coffee and chatted with the women. She finished, put the cup in a sink and went upstairs to see if she'd forgotten anything in room 35 before its scheduled guest arrived.

At forty-nine, Emma was exhausted after each day of maid work, but she had no choice. She and her husband, Benjaman, had worked a farm in Superior Township. It wasn't very lucrative, and they never did get enough money to buy it instead of just renting it. The farm work Emma had done there, helped by her only son, Loyd, was as tiring as cleaning rooms—but at least they could see the results of their work. When Benjaman died, Emma couldn't handle the farm by herself. She moved to town and applied for work at the hotel to support herself.

Emma and two other maids, Essie Freeman and another widow, Nellie Walling, kept the hotel's sixty rooms cleaned and made up. The manager, George Swanson, and the assistant manager, Richard MacFarlane, had been talking about adding two more floors to the hotel next year to create a total of one hundred rooms; Emma hoped that they'd add another maid or two as well.

Emma's most time-consuming job was cleaning the ten deluxe suites, which rented for $60.00 or $65.00 a week ($764.00 and $828.00 today). Next were the rooms with a private bathroom, at $2.50 and $3.00 per day ($32.00 and $38.00). Essie could zip through the cheaper rooms, at $1.50 and $1.75 ($19.00 and $22.00), which only offered access to a communal coin-operated lavatory down the hall.

Not two years later, the staff would be startled to see those lavatories mentioned in no less a publication than H.L. Mencken's *American Mercury* magazine. In the "Americana" section, a compilation of amusing tidbits culled from newspapers across the country, appeared one taken from an Ypsi paper: "A resident of Mason, Mich. is the nominee of George Swanson, manager of the Huron Hotel here, as Michigan's most honest citizen," the item read. "Swanson has a letter in which the Masonite encloses 25 cents with the explanation that he cheated the pay lavatory in the hotel three times while stopping at the Huron two years ago. Since then he has 'got the good old-fashioned religion,' he explained, and so encloses enough to cover the debt, plus interest."

Room 35 looked fine. Emma closed the door and headed for the stairs—just in time, as here came Lawrence, the new bellboy, with a suitcase, followed by a guest.

Lawrence Ollette's friends envied him his job, a glamorous one for a seventeen-year-old. He lived on Prospect Street with his thirty-seven-year-old mother, Cestia, his forty-year-old father, Bert, his younger brothers, Kenneth and Norvell, and his older sisters, Muriel and Hazel. Lawrence liked his job—he likely thought it better than Hazel's job as a stuffed toy stuffer in a toy factory. He worked with the other bellboy, eighteen-year-old Edmund Blair.

Lawrence opened the door to room 35 and set down the suitcase. The room seemed a little cold again this week. Perhaps he should tell Mr. Swanson to mention it to the hotel engineer, Alf LeCureux. Lawrence pointed out the room's bathroom, told the guest to call downstairs if he needed anything and smiled as he was handed a tip.

In addition to transient guests, the hotel also housed permanent lodgers. In 1930, it had ten, most of them single men. Edward Attyes was a fifty-five-year-old traveling salesman for a motor oil company. The twenty-six-year-old Terry Carney and the twenty-seven-year-old Ellis Benedict were traveling salesmen for a dry goods firm and for an investment company, respectively. The twenty-five-year-old Clayton Briggs also worked for an

Cornelia McLouth and Julia Jennings reenact pioneer ladies in front of the hotel during Ypsilanti's 1923 centennial. *Courtesy of Ypsilanti Archives.*

insurance company. The thirty-six-year-old World War I veteran Frank Schimel was a schoolteacher.

Also thirty-six, the divorced Elsa Freeman worked as a salesperson for a magazine company. Two married men, the twenty-eight-year-old Neal Routson and the thirty-nine-year-old World War I veteran Robert Heine, worked as a mechanic for a bus company and as a civil engineer for a paving company, respectively.

The last two lodgers were the sisters Ada and Gertrude Woodard. Seventy-four-year-old Ada was retired and lived at the hotel until her death. Fifty-nine-year-old Gertrude worked as a book indexer at the University of Michigan's law library. She was known in town as the first female driver in Washtenaw County. When she died, hotel staff found piles of yellowed papers reaching toward the ceiling of her quarters, with only narrow paths snaking in between.

After World War II, the hotel enjoyed a golden age, housing many air travelers who landed at Willow Run, then one of the nation's busiest airports. The hotel was almost full much of the time, and Cleary College, Eastern Michigan University and local organizations booked the dining rooms for formal events.

However, business began to decline in the early 1960s. The hotel's reign as the town's social hub ended in 1966, when six airlines were relocated from Willow Run Airport to Detroit Metro. The days of housing such guests as Truman's vice president, Alben Barkley, world-famous runner Paavo Nurmi and world-renowned black opera singer Marian Anderson were gone. Not long thereafter, the building ceased to be a hotel and was converted to office space. A series of first-floor restaurants occupied the old coffee shop space.

But in 1924, a modest crew of nineteen ordinary men and women, from various walks of life, maintained the elegant heart of downtown that the papers admiringly called "Ypsilanti's Waldorf-Astoria."

Part III

LATE NIGHT IN THE WORKSHOP

THE BATTERY-POWERED DEPOT

Batteries power our phones, tools, clocks, iPods, smoke detectors and sometimes our hearts. They came into widespread popular use only after World War II, and we tend to think of the prewar era, compared to modern days, as more or less battery-free. However, a century ago, the Ypsilanti Depot contained exactly one battery—a very important one.

Rail commuters approaching the depot from Depot Town around that time would first have seen the baggage room on the southern side of the structure. Residents were still adjusting to seeing the depot as a modest one-story red brick building, rebuilt after the 1910 fire that destroyed its former ornate splendor. Trunks and suitcases were stored inside the baggage room. Express mail offices handled packages and shipments.

An open, roofed-over space connected the baggage room and the depot's main building. Here, several heavy-duty handcarts were used to move trunks and packages on and off the trains.

Morning passengers gathered in the main building's waiting room. Despite the massive coal stove there, the waiting room was often "so chilly that the pail of drinking water with cup attached to a long chain was near freezing," recalled one old-timer. "Though the stenciled letters on the pail read 'Drinking Water Changed Hourly,' a goldfish could have lived undisturbed."

This old-timer was onetime Ypsilanti historian and retired blind linotype operator J. Milton Barnes. Two *Ypsi Press* articles in the Archives, one undated and one from May 13, 1979, feature his recollections of the early depot.

A 1919 view of the depot shows the onetime semaphore signal, whose arms' downward position signifies that the track is currently clear. *Courtesy of Ypsilanti Archives.*

Barnes continued: "With the crowd of morning commuters conversing or looking over recent acquisitions to the rack of timetables, the station master solemnly walked to the blackboard and chalked 'Train 207 (the Doodlebug) 10 minutes late.'"

A "Doodlebug" was a self-propelled, motorized, single railroad passenger car. It was useful to railroads because it could service small branch lines and short-distance routes under its own power without the hassle and expense of attaching a locomotive engine. In appearance and function, it was not unlike a slightly stretched-out interurban streetcar, except running on regular railroad tracks.

The waiting passengers, said Barnes, "could hear the telegraph instruments ticking and the relays' [amplifiers'] sound like echoes. We'd know that the Eastbound due at 6:55 had passed Ann Arbor. We could still make it to work on time."

That is, unless there was a late passenger sprinting for the eastbound train. "It happened at almost every stop," remembered Barnes, "and conductors were accustomed to being inveigled by station masters to delay for a moment…Here comes the laggard, hotfooting over the brick pavement between depot and waiting train. "'All Aboard!' The fireman would add a couple of shovels of Hocking Valley Lump [coal] to the engine's firebox because that 15 seconds of lost time must be made up and the train was due in Detroit in 28 minutes."

And there went the Detroit-bound train, curving out of sight and picking up speed. The emptied waiting room "wasn't like the ballroom floor after a dance, the janitor sweeping up crushed rose petals and confetti, a tiny program with chewed-off ear, a trampled ear-ring, a silken glove and a love-note torn to bits," Barnes said. "No! In Ypsilanti's Michigan Central Depot, after the conductor's 'All Aboard!' and two quick toots of the engine's whistle, the screams of compressed air, and the rollaway groans of the iron wheels, the Depotmaster made a quick survey. He erased from the blackboard 'North Shore—five minutes late' and chalked in 'Sunset Limited' and 'Motor City,' always 'on time'—till the telegraph clicks told different."

"Listen to the telegraph clicks! The Wabash is five minutes late coming into Detroit," Barnes continued. "Wabash? What has that train to do with the local Michigan Central trains? You might know! They'll hold the Sunset Limited in Detroit long enough for passengers to buy tickets."

The telegraph was the linchpin of the Michigan Central railroad system. Messages buzzing up and down the wire sent by the railroad's "lightning slingers" (telegraph operators) informed stations of schedule changes and tracked lost baggage.

The Michigan Central began installing a telegraph system in 1855 and was one of the first railroads to adopt this technology to coordinate trains. In the pre-telegraph days, operating a railroad was hazardous.

"When two trains which should have met and passed each other are more than half an hour behind their regular time, they must both proceed with the greatest caution, each sending a man with a flag, if in the daytime, or a red light by night, ahead around the curves," notes the 1852 MCRR rulebook. In Ypsilanti, factory girls commuting to work in Detroit, the family members waiting to greet a relative and travelers coordinating a trip depended on the depot telegraph.

The telegraph, in turn, depended on a giant five-gallon glass vat filled with liquid underneath the telegrapher's desk. At the bottom of the vat lay a copper plate and a pile of blue copper sulfate crystals. Near the top, a large zinc quarter-starburst resembling a crow's foot lay suspended horizontally in the liquid. Wires led from this "crowfoot battery" to the telegraph lines, powering the system.

Crowfoot batteries took advantage of electrochemical reactions between the metals, chemicals and liquid in the vat. The reactions threw off electrons that were siphoned off into wires and used to power telegraph messages.

The device produced one volt, less than tiny modern-day AAA batteries. But crowfoot batteries were ideal for appliances that required only an intermittent use, alternated with a downtime to recharge, such as the telegraph.

As a large vat of liquid, the "wet cell" was not portable but rather was well suited for stationary use in the depot. Crowfoot batteries were one of several types of wet cells used in telegraphy.

Barnes remembered the depot battery: "The clicks of the relay of the telegraph are mighty weak today. No wonder. The [liquid] is getting low in the big…five gallon glass battery under the instrument bench, with the enormous zinc crowfoot and its copper shield. Bring it to life. Needs another lump of blue vitriol [copper sulfate]."

Like cellphones and other handheld devices, Ypsilanti's depot telegraph was also a high-tech battery-powered communications device a century ago.

THE 1926 MODEM

In the fall of 1925, Ypsilantians, and the nation, were transfixed by the romance of a onetime Lower East Side immigrant kid and a telegraph magnate's daughter. Her wealthy father, Clarence, the son of Comstock Lode multimillionaire John Mackay, strongly disapproved of his Catholic daughter Ellin's interest in a Jewish man with what he viewed as a disreputable occupation. Clarence refused to give Ellin his permission to marry. The couple waited in dismay for Clarence to change his mind.

Daily Ypsilantian-Press editor George Handy waited as well for the next tidbit of news—his readers loved the story. When in January 1926 that news came from New York, it was a bombshell. Ellin Mackay had eloped with and married Irving Berlin.

Handy needed a wedding photograph from New York and fast—this story was too big to wait for the mail. He called New York. Half an hour later, he had a photograph, thanks to the only modem in Ypsilanti in 1926. That modem, half the size of a refrigerator, stood in the *Press*'s building at 101–105 North Huron. Called a "telephotography" machine, it could receive photographs from telegraph wires.

Telegraphy had a long history in Ypsilanti. The first telegraphic message sent in Michigan traveled from the Detroit telegraph office at Jefferson and Cass Avenues in Detroit to Ypsilanti's railroad depot on November 29, 1847, through lines strung along the Michigan Central railroad tracks.

The first message sent by the "lightning slingers" was not without a hint of playful glee. Detroit sent first: "Detroit presents her compliments to her sister, Ypsilanti, who never promises more than she is willing and able to perform. Our connection by lightning is now complete, and the first flash in Michigan conveying intelligent messages has passed between us; may our 'current' never be broken, our 'batteries' always in order, and our 'registers' ready at all times to tell the truth, the whole truth, and nothing but the truth."

Ypsilanti replied: "Ypsilanti [-.---.---. . . . .. .-.. .- -.---..] reciprocates the kind wishes of our lovely sister, Detroit, and as we are now not only on speaking terms, but within speaking distance, she hopes that our intercourse by lightning may be pleasant and profitable to both. So mote it [so be it]."

Continuing from the telegraph station in Ypsilanti, this "Erie and Michigan" line reached Chicago in the winter of 1848. But it wouldn't be until many years later that photographs began flying along the wires.

In the 1920s, "telephotography" was not new. As early as 1895, the *San Francisco Call* newspaper received a simple line drawing, sent by telegraph, of a Los Angeles parade. The message consisted of an alphanumeric code indicating grid coordinates of the drawing's line segments. The telegrapher also cabled a text description of the parade. An artist at the *Call* used the description to sketch details onto the line drawing, creating a detailed picture. The next morning, the paper printed a timely image of the Los Angeles event.

Telephotography made newspapers look up-to-the-minute. The technology was also used in law enforcement. Criminals' pictures could be circulated in minutes, before the lawbreakers traveled too far. Their fingerprints could also be sent by wire. In 1922, the *New York Times* called telephotography "that Nemesis of Malefactors." The speed of information transmission was beginning its long, dramatic and world-changing acceleration.

The modem at the *Ypsi Press* consisted of a cylindrical metal drum and a tiny pinpoint flashlight within its cabinet. It was hooked up to a telegraph wire. So was another similar machine, a transmitter, in New York.

In New York, a worker wrapped a photograph around the transmitter cylinder. When the machine was turned on, a tiny beam of light shone on the photo as the cylinder rotated about one hundred times per minute, slowly advancing along a threaded axis. The transmitter scanned the photo in one-hundredth-inch sections at one hundred lines to the inch; each square inch had ten thousand bits of information.

As the beam of slight scanned a slow spiral down the moving cylinder, a receptor caught the reflection of either dark or light areas of the photo. A photosensitive component translated the "dark" and "light" reflections into differing pulses of electricity. This coded electrical signal was telegraphed to Ypsilanti. The New York transmitter could send, and the Ypsi receiver could receive, 1,800 bits of information per second. A five-by-seven photo could be sent and received in about seven minutes.

In Ypsilanti, the receiver machine, whose rotation was adjusted to exactly match that of the New York machine, decoded the electrical signal back into information indicating light and dark areas. The receiver shone light of corresponding strength onto a fresh piece of photographic film attached to the cylinder.

In this way, a photo negative was produced, which was then developed and used in the Ypsi paper. The resulting photo had a more limited tonal range than the original. Also, someone had blocked out most of the background in white to highlight the married couple. Nevertheless, the photo contained an astounding amount of data.

That 1,800 bits per second is faster than the first commercial modem, AT&T's 1962 Bell 103, which transmitted at 300 bits per second (bps). At this time, 300 bits per second equaled 300 baud, the unit of modem speed. Later, computer scientists figured out how to pack more bits into each baud, and bps became a more descriptive term for modem speed.

As much as we associate modems with the term "baud," the term actually comes from telegraphy. Named to honor the French inventor who created the first teleprinter, J.M.E. Baudot, one "baud" is a unit of telegraph speed consisting of one Morse code dot sent per second.

Since that 1926 day when the *Press* received its New York photo, time has moved on. The telephotography machine became an obsolete clunker. Irving Berlin's father-in-law eventually forgave him and accepted their marriage—all the better for him, since Irving would stay married to Ellin for sixty-two years, until her death in 1988. Berlin died the following year, shortly before the popularization of dial-up modems, like the one that had transmitted his happy wedding picture all those years ago.

Forgotten Phones

Quiz a friend or two about who popularized the type of electricity we use today—go ahead, get your geek on—and a few would correctly name Nikola Tesla. Then ask who invented long-distance telephony. Probably no one would answer correctly.

It wasn't Alexander Graham Bell, Thomas Edison or any other celebrated name from the late nineteenth century's feverish and fertile age of invention. Like his renowned contemporary, Tesla, the inventor of long-distance telephony was an electrical engineer. Unlike Tesla's numerous, sophisticated and lasting inventions, his were few, crude and transient. But they worked, and they brought him temporary fame.

Just as Tesla's brilliance and legacy weren't fully appreciated until long after his death, so also should be remembered the legacy of his humbler brother inventor whose name once graced the *New York Times*: Ypsilanti engineer Webster Gillett.

Born in about 1840, Webster, his older brother, Charles, and younger sister, Alma, grew up on their parents' 80-acre farm just east of Ypsilanti. Webster's father, Jason, kept a few milk cows and pigs and a small flock of sheep. He raised wheat, Indian corn and oats. Jason was a hardworking farmer. Between 1850 and 1870, his farm grew in size from 80 to 135 acres, and its value rose from $1,000 to $10,000 ($170,000 today). He was one of the more successful farmers in his neighborhood.

In about 1870, Jason's twenty-nine-year-old son, Webster, also found success. He was granted the first of what would be nine patents, for an electric alarm for use on railroad cars. Soon after, he obtained another, for an electrical temperature signal. The device received a mention in the November 9, 1872 issue of the *Telegrapher* magazine, published in New York.

A year later, at age thirty-three, Webster was superintendent of Ypsilanti's Northwestern Telegraph Manufacturing Company. The company made and sold "Gillett's Telegraph Apparatus, Gillett's Electrical Railway Signals, Gillett's Electrical Temperature Signals," as well as "Gillett's Hotel Enunciator."

Webster started his career in an Ypsilanti telegraph supply company. The hotel enunciator, also called "annunciator," was similar to a hospital call-button system. Hotel guests could use it to summon room service. Webster was not the first to invent an enunciator, but his work on a device for communication over distance presaged his work to come.

In about 1880, at age forty, Webster began his most important and productive period of work. Between March 1879 and the fall of 1880, he was granted three patents: for a method of adapting telegraph lines for telephone transmission and for two versions of a speaking telephone (just a few years after Bell's original telephone patent). Webster assigned one half of one telephone patent to Brooklyn engineer Richard Schermerhorn. He said farewell to his parents on the farm and moved to New York City.

Considering that the telephone is a direct outgrowth of the telegraph, it's unsurprising that Webster got involved in a telephone equipment company in his new home of Brooklyn. He wasn't alone in doing so. Telephony was the cutting-edge technology of the day, and many inventors were contributing ideas. There was only one technological problem that even Alexander Graham Bell couldn't solve: long-distance calls.

Telephony works by creating an electrical wave whose shape mirrors the sound wave of a speaker's voice. At the receiving end, the electrical signal is converted back into a sound wave, producing recognizable speech. The only problem, in Webster's day, was that the electrical signal was weak and, upon encountering resistance in the wire, soon petered out.

An obvious solution would be to provide a stronger electrical current from the transmitting end to push the signal farther. This wasn't possible—too much current burned out the delicate needle-and-diaphragm apparatus that converted sound into an electrical wave.

Webster created a mechanical solution to this electrical problem. He simply added more needle-diaphragm pairs, each with its own battery power supply. First he invented a "two-point" (two needle-diaphragms) telephone. This instantly doubled the power pushing the signal down the line. He next created a four-point and a ten-point telephone. His crowning achievement was the twenty-point telephone.

This baroque device contained what resembled a candelabra of twenty needles and diaphragms. A voice speaking into the telephone made all twenty needles quiver. Each needle was wired to its own independent battery. The powerful combined signal surged much farther down the wires than ever before.

The December 20, 1883 *New York Times* reported:

> *Experiments were made last night on the large wire of the Postal Telegraph Company between New York and Meadville, Penn., a distance of 500 miles, with a telephone devised by Prof. Webster Gillett, of Ypsilanti, Mich.*

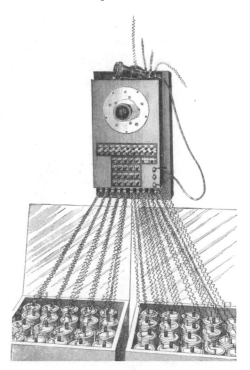

Exterior view of Gillett's twenty-point telephone and its batteries, two per needle. *Author's collection.*

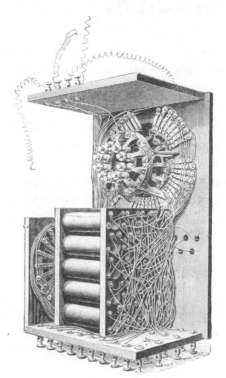

An interior view of the telephone looking from the rear shows the circular array of needles and points surrounding the mouthpiece. *Author's collection.*

At the New York end of the wire were Prof. Gillett [and] Judge E.R. Wiggins, of Boston, the President of the Atlantic and Pacific Telephone Company, which owns the patents…Alfred Beal was at the Meadville end…there was little difficulty in carrying on a conversation. The gentlemen here held receivers to their ears, while Mr. Beal addressed them and sang "Way Down Upon the Swanee River" and "Old Black Joe," which came plainly over the wire. Prof. Gillett asked Mr. Beal for a piece of his wedding cake. Judge Wiggins said he could hear Mr. Beal blush. The provocation for the blush was listening in Meadville.

What Prof. Gillett calls a 10-point instrument was used. He uses in his transmitter a needle attached to a rubber disc…Each point, Prof. Gillett says, is like adding another telephone in power…"We feel confident that before we get through we are going to say 'Hello' and a good deal more, too, to the people on the other side," said Prof. Gillett. "What we are aiming at is communication at long distances."

Webster's aim was true. Before long, his innovation enabled a call from New York to Chicago's famed meatpacking titan, Philip Armour. The question that came over the wire to Mr. Armour, according to the February 6, 1885 *New York Times*, was: "Is it true that Chicago girls have big feet?"

"With painful deliberation," reported the *Times*, "[the caller] spoke this query into a little transmitter of one of Webster Gillett's long-distance telephones last night. The agitated diaphragm passed the interrogation on to one of the Postal Telegraph Company's wires, and on the copper highway it sped on to Chicago."

What the paper called the "eminent pork expert," Philip Armour, "pondered long, and finally answered sorrowfully, 'They have.'"

Advances in telephone equipment soon made Webster's intricate phones obsolete. His name is absent from encyclopedias and telephone histories. But for a moment in the 1880s, the Ypsilanti inventor, whose sheer brainpower whisked him from a humble farm to a cosmopolitan city and won him momentary fame, was at the forefront of long-distance technology.

An Automatic Toast-Butterer

Ypsilanti has a long history of forgotten inventions. Black Canadian-born inventor Elijah McCoy's railroad lubricating cup is locally well known, his lawn sprinkler and folding ironing board less so. Some locals recall that Alva

Worden created a whip-socket, a cylindrical clamp attached to the front of a wagon in which the driver could conveniently store his horsewhip. Forgotten are his horse net and his "instrument for stretching elastic gaiters."

Some decades after these men, during the Depression, Ypsilantian Robert Roy Dickerson invented an automatic "toast buttering device" in what may have been one ordinary man's attempt to secure wealth and fame.

The oldest son of Willis, Michigan merchant Charles Dewitt Dickerson and his wife, Judith Fountain Dickerson, Robert grew up in modest circumstances. About the time he attended high school, the family moved to a home on Ypsilanti's Summit Street. Robert attended Normal College and graduated in 1913 with a degree in manual arts. He was not an athletic student but participated in the Young Men's Christian Association, the fraternity Alpha Tau Delta and the Crafts Club, as well as was treasurer of the oratory club. His unsmiling senior picture in the 1913 Normal College yearbook suggests a steady, serious young man.

Robert married Hazel Kelly a year after he graduated, and the couple left town for California. Robert became a school principal and later a superintendent in the newly settled southern California city of Imperial. Their first child, Mark, was born in 1915.

In 1917, Robert registered for the World War I draft. His draft card says that he was a tall man of medium build, with blue eyes and light hair; he was also "not bald." He was never drafted. Robert and Hazel had two more children, Robert Jr. in 1917 and Phyllis in 1919, after which the family returned to Ypsilanti.

It appears that Robert's parents gave or sold him the Summit Street home upon his return. His parents moved to 509 Forest, where they ran a boardinghouse. In 1922, Robert opened a small restaurant in the home, at 235 North Summit near the water tower. Hazel worked as a cook and in 1922 gave birth to the couple's fourth and final child, Charles. When the Depression began with the stock market crash in October 1929, the effect on Ypsilanti wasn't immediate. By 1931, however, the local situation had worsened. That year, Robert invented his toast-buttering device.

Made of ninety-four separate metal parts, and about the size and shape of a desktop printer, the electrical device contained a reservoir of melted butter and an overhanging rack supporting several pieces of toast. In his patent application, Robert said that "an object of the invention is to provide a simple and comparatively inexpensive device in which slices of

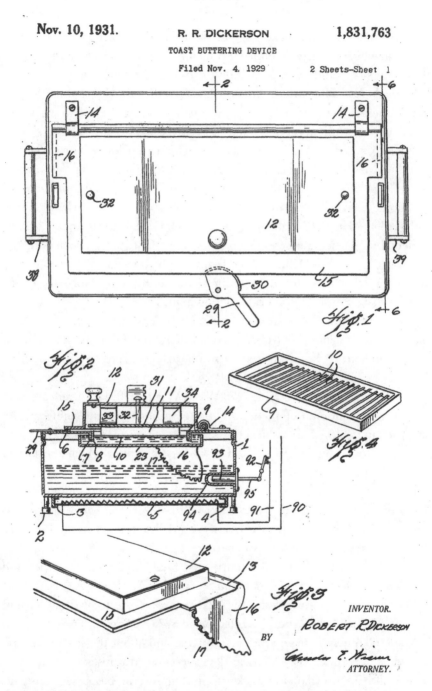

Dickerson's patent drawing for his toast-butterer shows, from top, a top-down view of the device, the toast tray, a side cutaway view of the butter reservoir and part of the lid. *Author's collection.*

toasted bread for instance may be positioned and by a simple manipulation or leverage device [the machine could] raise a tray carrying melted butter [from the reservoir] to contact with one side of the toast."

Robert thought highly of his intricate toast-butterer. His patent was granted, and he immediately incorporated as the Dickerson Butterfaster Company. The 1931 city directory lists his occupation no longer as restaurant owner but rather as "salesman," likely for the toast-butterer. He probably hoped to initially sell the device to the two dozen other small restaurants in town, which included the Wolverine Café at 207 West Michigan Avenue, the Ypsi Lunch at 2 North Huron and the stylish orange-and-black-themed coffee shop at the Huron Hotel (now the Centennial Center) at Pearl and Washington.

Despite his efforts, he failed to sell his toast-butterer. Perhaps by 1931, Ypsilantians were eating out less, and restaurateurs had less discretionary money. It also may be that the issue of speedy toast-buttering was less pressing than Robert had imagined and that he had invented a solution for a nonexistent problem.

Robert abandoned his toast-butterer and his restaurant and, in 1932, opened the Tower Grocery Store, also at 235 Summit. In an era before large supermarkets, there were thirty-four other small grocers in town who delivered groceries to homes. Competing with them were the cheaper, upstart "cash and carry" outlets of A&P and Kroger's, which would later expand, compete and outdo the traditional small grocers. From the Tower Grocery, Robert could watch the construction of the Ethel Terrace apartments across the street (now Flo-Mar Apartments). He witnessed many other changes in town as well, since the Tower Grocery stayed open until Robert, at age sixty, sold it in 1950 to Thomas Theodoris. Theodoris tried to continue the little grocery but closed it after just a few years.

Robert vanishes from city directories by 1954. He is apparently not buried either at Highland Cemetery or the Dickerson family plot in Ypsilanti Township's Union-Udell Cemetery, although his daughter, Phyllis, the last of Robert's children to pass away, was buried there in 2008. It may be that Robert returned to California to live with his son, Robert Jr., who was a minister there.

Robert was an ordinary man with a humble dream of popularizing a restaurant appliance. Though he failed, his toast-butterer is a reminder of all of the ordinary, unsung Ypsilantians with the imagination and perseverance to create something new.

The DIY Ice Saw

Ypsilanti once had horses that walked on water. They pulled a plow over the surface of the Huron River. Men with long saws watched, waiting their turn to work.

From the late nineteenth century until the winter of 1922, the Michigan Central railroad maintained an ice-cutting station just northeast of Ypsilanti, behind today's St. Joseph Hospital and near an old gravel pit called Shanghai Pit.

In winter, the railroad hired men to cut ice from the river. Horses pulling a sort of plow scraped lines on the ice, which were then cut into blocks with handsaws. The blocks were floated to shore, pushed by men with long pikes. Each twelve-to fifteen-inch-thick block weighed well over one hundred pounds.

For decades, it was dangerous and exhausting work, until in 1920 Ypsilantian Charles McKie had an idea. Thirty-three-year-old Charles was a self-employed interior decorator. He was tall and slender, with blue eyes and brown hair. He painted and decorated the interiors of Ypsilanti offices. Charles owned a home at 213 Huron, where he lived with his wife, Dee, and his mother, Martha. One next-door neighbor was Normal school music professor and violinist A.J. Whitmire. Nearby lived pastor Harvey Colburn, who would soon write the book for which he is remembered today, *The Story of Ypsilanti.*

Charles was friends with Lee Dawson, who with other family members ran the Martin Dawson Company, which dealt in hay, grain, seeds, coal and building and painting supplies. Dawson had the contract for cutting ice for the Michigan Central Railroad.

Charles's idea took him to the Wiedman auto dealership on Pearl Street, at the present-day bus station. He obtained four old Model Ts. The body of each car was cut off and the wheels removed, leaving just the gas engines and the drive trains to the back axle. Charles mounted each engine on a wooden frame with sled runners. Where the rear wheels had been, Charles mounted two forty-eight-inch-wide saw blades. The Model Ts were now ice saws.

Transported to Shanghai Pit, they roared to life, with a racketing four-cylinder, twenty-horsepower engine and a spray of ice chips thrown up by the blade. They worked so well that although Charles had made four, the ice harvesters only needed one to get the work done. A wooden frame

McKie's ice saw was created long before Michigan's OSHA department. *Courtesy of Ypsilanti Archives.*

supporting what appears in a photo to be a leather screen was added where the windshield had been, to shield the operator from flying ice.

Pushed to shore, the ice blocks traveled up a wooden ramp on a conveyor belt powered by a steam engine that Dawson had rented. They were stored in the railroad's Ypsilanti icehouses along the Huron and loaded onto boxcars for storage in the railroad's icehouse in Detroit. Stored in sawdust for insulation, the blocks were used to cool boxcars. "The Michigan Central Railroad Company is filling its ice houses at Ypsilanti with fine ice from Shanghai Pond," said the February 1910 issue of *Cold Storage and Ice Trade Journal.* "It is fifteen inches thick."

Some of the ice likely was used in Ypsilanti as well. Around the turn of the century, about half of American households had iceboxes. These small wooden cabinets lined with tin or zinc had a storage space for a block of ice and shelves on which to keep food cool. Ypsilantians who couldn't afford an icebox and the regular home delivery of ice blocks about twice a week could store food in a cool cellar, or do without.

Although the MCRR's ice-harvesting site was upstream of waste-generating paper mills and other factories, there are hints that the Huron River ice was polluted. The MCRR claimed that it only used northern Michigan ice for consumption in its dining cars. It used Ypsi ice only to cool boxcars.

In 1919, train inspectors were alarmed to see the quality of Ypsilanti water. "[G]overnment inspectors of a train passing through Ypsilanti saw water running from a hose at the Michigan Central Gardens," noted the July 24 *Daily Ypsilantian-Press*. The men tested the water for purity. "The test was very bad and orders were immediately issued forbidding use of Ypsilanti [city] water." Later, the inspectors found that the hose was not drawing city water, which came from a well, but rather polluted river water near a sewer outlet.

Demand for clean ice drove the creation of artificial ice-making factories. In 1906, Wyandotte's Eureka Brewing Company began manufacturing artificial ice. In 1909, Ann Arbor founded the Artificial Ice Company. Detroit's General Ice Delivery Company and other Detroit companies began making ice as well. In 1918, the Wyandotte Ice Company followed. In 1919, the Ypsi Pure Ice Company advertised in the *Daily Ypsilantian-Press*: "Our new artificial ice plant is now in operation and we are prepared to supply ice to all consumers in Ypsilanti and vicinity."

Artificial ice was clean, could be made in precise sizes and could be made year round without reliance on unpredictable weather. Except for isolated rural areas far from artificial ice plants, the age of ice harvesting was over.

Perhaps Charles might have made a business out of building and shipping his ice saw to northern ice-harvesting sites. Soon after the collapse of local ice harvesting, his own life took a downturn. He and Dee divorced. She remained in the Huron house, apparently alone; there is no census record of their having had children.

Charles eventually moved into Lee Dawson's house at 214 South Hamilton. Charles no longer worked as an interior decorator but rather at the less prestigious job of outdoor sign painter. His neighbors were laborers, domestics and factory hands, including Harry Brothers, an auto stripper in an auto factory, and foundry worker Newton Cary.

Although artificial ice factories made Charles's invention obsolete, it would have happened eventually. A very few expensive models of electric home refrigerators were produced in the 1930s and became more widely available after World War II.

Men cutting ice on the Huron River, with a train in the background and three ice saws visible. *Courtesy of Ypsilanti Archives.*

Today, the only places to see iceboxes are antique shops and museums. The Ypsilanti Historical Museum has one in its kitchen. It's just barely possible that its ice compartment once held a block of ice cut by a young man, gleeful at the controls of his loud, dangerous invention, all those years ago.

Faint Footprints

Swastika slippers made in Ypsilanti were once openly advertised in national magazines—including *Cosmopolitan*. In its day, the footwear didn't cause outrage or taint the city as sympathetic to Nazis—even though two other Ypsi companies made similar items.

The swastika slipper was made in the Indian Shoe Company's little third-floor factory at 17–21 Cross Street, above the present-day Fantasy Attic costume store. In the high-ceilinged space full of light from large south-facing windows sat an array of shoemaking machines with tough, leather-penetrating needles, operated by about a dozen women and a few men.

Benjamin Boyce managed the company but soon moved on to become the bookkeeper for the Peninsular Paper Mill. His lengthy December 12,

Genuine Indian House Shoes
(Ypsilanti Moosehide)

$2 Post-paid

For indoors or out, the most comfortable shoes you ever wore —the latest in high grade foot-ease. Ypsilanti Moosehide is tough but pliable, heavy yet very flexible. Guaranteed to wear and to satisfy for years, being **INDIAN SEWED.** Burnt and tinted designs—over a score for men, women and children at **FACTORY PRICES.** Men's (size 5½ to 10) or Ladies' (size 2½ to 7), $2; Babies' (size 3 to 8), $1. **ORDER TODAY,** stating size, or write for folder of 1910 styles.

YPSILANTI INDIAN SHOE CO., 30 E. Cross St., Ypsilanti, Mich.

A 1910 model featured a prominent design. *Author's collection.*

1956 *Ypsilanti Daily Press* obituary makes no mention of his involvement with the Indian Shoe Company.

During Boyce's tenure there, the company's 1910 Depot Town neighbors included Charles Dueress's grocery store, King and Pressler's secondhand shop, Pearl Laundry, the business office for the underwear factory, C.M. Fairchild & Company's flour and feed store, coal dealer John Engel's office and the Oliver House hotel. The district was bustling and noisy, with trains frequently pulling in and out of the depot area on multiple parallel tracks.

The Indian Shoe Company made moccasins from scratch, starting with cured hides that may have come from the Ypsilanti Hide and Leather Company, John Howland's odiferous tannery. "The smell coming from that place is intolerable, especially in the evening when there is but a slight breeze," noted the July 14, 1909 *Ypsilanti Daily Press*, quoting a "prominent Forest Avenue matron." That matron may have pulled a rawhide string or two, as Howland soon after moved his tannery from Forest Avenue to 25 South Huron at the south edge of the commercial district.

After delivery to the Indian Shoe Company, the skins were cut into pieces using patterns. Finished sizes ranged from 3½ to 10 for men and 2½ to 7 for women, along with children's sizes. Many of the moccasins were decorated with designs made with colored ink or a leather-burning tool. The designs incorporated what the company judged to be Native American motifs.

One 1910 model featured a large swastika on the toe. The Indian Shoe Company likely chose this design due to its traditional use as a decorative motif by the Navaho, Hopi and other indigenous peoples, long before the symbol acquired its indelible association with genocide during World War II.

The completed moccasins sold by mail for two dollars (forty-six dollars in 2010 currency). "[T]he most comfortable shoe you ever wore—the latest in high grade foot-ease," noted one 1910 ad, which claimed that the shoes were made of a material it called "Ypsilanti Moosehide." "Ypsilanti Moosehide is tough but pliable," it argued, "heavy yet very flexible. Guaranteed to wear and to satisfy for years, being INDIAN SEWED."

A full-page 1913 ad in the outdoorsman's publication *Outing* magazine went further, touting the shoes as perfect for a range of outdoor and indoor

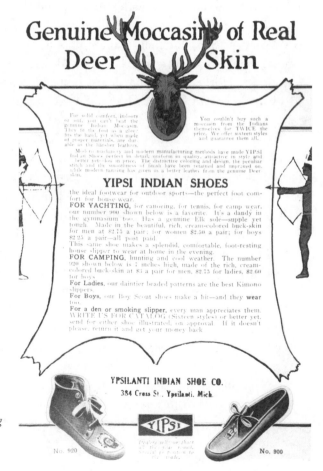

The full-page ad in *Outing* magazine touted the moccasins' many uses. *Author's collection.*

uses. It was, for instance, an ideal yachting moccasin. "[F]or canoeing, for tennis, for camp wear, our number 900 shown below is a favorite," noted the ad. "It's a dandy in the gymnasium, too…[and for] camping, hunting, and cool weather…This same shoe makes a splendid, comfortable, foot-resting house slipper to wear at home in the evening." By this time, the Indian Shoe Company had devised a logo, consisting of the word "YIPSI" in a horizontal diamond—presumably with the extra "I" so that out-of-town customers wouldn't wonder how to pronounce the strange four-letter word.

Perhaps the oddest aspect of the Indian Shoe Company's story is that it was one of three moccasin companies in Washtenaw County—none of which operated in the county's largest city. By about 1910, Ann Arbor had nearly twenty shoemaking shops, including Justice Houghtalin's shop on Liberty, the Walk-Over Shoe Company on Main and Clark & Cooch ("Bang-Up Shoes for Boys") with stores on both Forest Avenue and South University. All three moccasin manufactories, however, were in Ypsilanti.

In Ypsi in 1906, Sumner Damon founded the Elk Skin Moccasin Manufacturing Company at 11 North Huron. A year later, Thomas McAndrew's Horner Specialty Shoe Company began making moccasins and athletic shoes. In 1909, the Indian Shoe Company was the last to arrive on Ypsi's bustling moccasin manufacturing scene.

"During the past few years the 'Indian fad' has taken the country almost by storm," wrote O.H. Kipps in a 1906 edition of *Southern Workman* magazine. "There has been a great demand for all sorts of Indian handiwork…Indian purses and moccasins…have been placed upon the market by enterprising dealers." It may be that the three Ypsi companies were formed to capitalize on this so-called Indian fad. However, the demand for such goods eventually faded.

The Indian Shoe Company went out of business just a few years after its opening. The Horner Specialty Shoe Company, which for a while shared factory space with the Indian Shoe Company, was also closed. For a while in the 1920s before it, too, went out of business, the Elk Skin company became the third moccasin manufacturer to occupy the Cross Street space—making that space the unrivaled historical hot spot of moccasin manufacturing in all of Washtenaw County.

Now apartments, the Depot Town space is all that remains. Aside from an obscure ad or two in forgotten publications and a few listings in city directories, Ypsilanti's early twentieth-century era of locally handcrafted moccasins vanished, leaving no footprint.

Earth Closets

In the late nineteenth century, two University of Michigan professors of medicine and an Ypsilanti doctor championed a new sanitation technology. Despite their efforts spanning nearly twenty years, the earth closet turned out to be arguably the least enthusiastically adopted invention in Michigan history.

It was an era of primitive indoor toilets connected to odiferous privy vaults—if you were lucky. Even elegant urban houses had backyard outhouses, such as Ann Arbor's historic Kempf House.

Patented in England in 1873 by Henry Moule, the earth closet resembled a wooden box with a backrest containing a metal hopper. The hopper was filled with clean, dry dirt. After using this commode, the user turned a tiny handle that dropped a small portion of dirt into the pail, covering its contents and rendering them allegedly odor-free. In time, the pail was removed and emptied, often on one's garden. Lower-tech earth closets without a hopper had a bucket of dirt nearby on the floor. It was a nineteenth-century composting toilet.

University of Michigan professor of medicine (and future medical school dean) Alonzo Palmer published "Dry Earth as a Means of Disposal of Excreta" in the September 1870 edition of the *Michigan University Medical Journal.*

The paper's first sentence read, "In Nutrition, considered in the largest sense—in the maintenance of the body—in the selection and appropriation of proper nutrient particles and the rejection of others, and in the renewal of tissues so constantly occurring, rejected and worn out materials in a state ready to undergo decomposition are constantly being expelled from the body by its various emunctories [excretory organs]."

Palmer went on to list cases of typhoid and enteric fever around the country and abroad. He discussed their link to unsanitary privies, cesspools and contaminated drinking water. He opined that the earth closet would "afford a comfortable closet on any floor of the house, which may be supplied with earth and cleansed of its deposits, without annoyance or inconvenience—a portable commode, in any dressing room, bedroom or closet, the care of which is no more disagreeable than that of a stove."

"The remedy," he said, "consists in mingling with dry and porous earth immediately all excreta. In so doing its particles are brought so in contact with the substance of the earth as to effect chemical changes, rendering the matters inoffensive and innoxious, preparing them for entering vegetable organisms as a part of their proper nutrient pabulum."

Palmer invoked Biblical authority. "This is no newly discovered principle or modern practice. It was enjoined by Moses as an important hygienic measure, when [in] Deuteronomy 23:12 and 13 a paddle was directed to be provided for each weapon, to be used [as a shovel for waste burial]."

He warned of the folly—even danger—of wasting valuable excreta. "[Ancient Rome's] Cloaca Maxima [a sewer, whose patron goddess was Cloacina]…carrying the waste of that great city into the Mediterranean, by the impoverishment of the soil, has been regarded as among the chief causes of the fall of the Empire."

Palmer's talk was an outgrowth of the era's heightened awareness of the value of sanitation. Ten years later, Michigan would hold its first statewide Sanitary Convention. It became an annual event held in cities around the state.

At the July 1, 1885 state Sanitary Convention, held in Ypsilanti that year, local doctor Ruth French opened the proceedings with her talk on the "Management of Earth Closets."

"Perhaps to some the subject of this paper may seem very unimportant," she began, "but to those who are interested in the health and general welfare of the people, it has been from the earliest times a matter of sufficient importance to demand legislation." Like Palmer, she made reference to Moses. She also enumerated the advantages of earth closets.

- *They do away with all offensive odor.*
- *They prevent contamination of soil, and consequently water, thereby preventing the cause of much sickness and death.*
- *They can be placed under the same roof as the house, so as to be easily accessible for women, children and invalids, in stormy and cold weather.*
- *In cases of typhoid, cholera, and other diseases, propagated through the evacuations, by first disinfecting with copperas, then treating with dry earth, there is no possible opportunity for harm to come from them if kept in a dry place, for a short time.*

Possibly inspired in part by the Sanitary Convention's publicity of the subject, in the same year William Heap and two colleagues established Michigan's first (and last) earth closet factory. Heap's Muskegon firm manufactured earth closets and piano stools. The company advertised its earth closets until at least 1891 but ceased making them before the new century. Heap shifted to making flush toilets, later giving the business to his son.

Other Michiganders were tinkering with the devices. At least four earth closet–related patents were filed by inventors in Lansing, Grand Rapids, Carson City and Centreville between 1871 and 1895.

In an April 1, 1887 edition of the semimonthly magazine the *Sanitary Era*, University of Michigan professor and later medical school dean Victor Vaughan addressed the issue: "A dry-earth closet properly kept is free from all noxious gases, and there is no possibility of the drinking water being contaminated by it."

But it seems likely that the volume of dirt required year round and the work of keeping the pail clean was regarded by average Michiganders as just too much trouble. Despite the efforts of the three local doctors and others, the device's end came soon.

Four years after Vaughan's article, Ypsilanti began installing its first municipal sewer system, with Ann Arbor following suit in 1893. In each city, the old unsanitary privy vaults were emptied, filled with fresh soil and sealed shut. Flush toilets with water traps eliminated the old problem of sewer gas in the home. Disease rates fell. And the earth closet became history.

Part IV

SERVANTS' QUARTERS

THE COLDWATER DOLL

Thirteen-year-old Ida ran upstairs into the bedroom and opened the closet. Such beautiful things—skirts, dresses and blouses—but which one to pick? She selected a long brown skirt of light, glossy brilliantine and a brown wool shirt stitched in red silk. They would look lovely with Ida's brown hair. The clothes were too large but were so much nicer than the drab blouse, faded blue skirt and worn, over-the-ankle black shoes that she had on. There wasn't much time, so she quickly changed.

"Ida!" called a woman from downstairs. "Suppertime!"

It was the eve of Halloween in 1905, but Ida wasn't selecting a costume or playing dress-up before Saturday dinner. She was planning an escape. Although she lived with Mr. and Mrs. Curson* in Ypsilanti's prosperous Normal Park, she wasn't their daughter or even a relative. Ida's relatives had abandoned her.

That night, her place at the table remained empty. Local newspapers in Ypsilanti and Ann Arbor later pieced together the story. Ida walked downtown and took the 5:45 p.m. interurban to Ann Arbor. She went to Mack's, a large department store on South Main Street, and bought a fancy collar and an elaborate hat. Then Ida traveled to Detroit and checked herself into a hotel near the downtown Campus Martius area. She used up about $10 (about $240 today), which she'd taken from the Curson home.

The next day, Ida went shopping in Detroit. She bought a plain, unclothed doll, a fancy shawl for it and a length of silk intended for doll clothes. For herself, she bought three hair combs, a pair of gloves and some ribbons. On Sunday night, she checked back into the hotel.

On Monday evening, local papers later said, Ida started back to Ann Arbor, where she'd seen a "help wanted" sign. She got as far as Ypsi before tiring out at 10:00 p.m. Disembarking at Ypsi, she was recognized by interurban agents.

Ida was hard to overlook. Not only were her fancy clothes (sized for a grown woman) ill-fitting for a thirteen-year-old girl, she also wore them strangely. Her blouse flopped loosely outside her skirt instead of being neatly tucked in, according to the custom of the day. Her new collar looked incongruous, and her elaborate hat was suitable for a fifty-year-old society matron. "[T]he manner of donning the dress was, if modish, decidedly new to Ypsilanti," joked the October 31 *Ypsilanti Daily Press*, calling it "recherché."

There was a reason, unexplored by the newspaper stories, why Ida wanted beautiful things and why she had no idea of how to wear them. She was a Coldwater girl.

Located in Branch County's town of Coldwater, Coldwater State Public School was Michigan's institution for abandoned children, or those without resources. Established in 1871 by a legislative act and opened in 1874, the school took in children from disadvantaged backgrounds. Some were children living in—and sometimes born in—county poorhouses. Some had mental deficiencies or behavioral disorders that some families, given the scant resources of the day, found too difficult to handle or else thought that the public school could better address to help their child. Officials had taken some children from families judged unfit. And some, like Ida, were those whose foster placement with relatives had failed—Ida's aunt and uncle had sent her to the school.

When she arrived, the school consisted of 160 acres, with an elegant Second Empire administration building, nine "cottages" for the children, a school, a chapel, a dining room, a hospital and a working farm.

Coldwater wasn't meant to be residential. It allowed children to be adopted out or contracted out under a work indenture plan, with both the school and the child receiving payment. The school's agents, one for each Michigan county, logged much time on the train assessing the homes of those who'd requested a child, checking up on previously placed children and transporting children from bad situations to Coldwater.

By the time Ida arrived at Coldwater in about 1904, 5,790 children had been received at the school since its opening, according to Henry Collins's

1906 history of Branch County. Of these children, 1,207 were indentured out, 687 were legally adopted, 589 were restored to their parents, 749 were returned to their home counties, 360 were aged out, 186 were married, 172 remained in Coldwater and 1,613 became self-supporting. Roughly 1 in 25—a total of 227—had died, either at the school or at the host home.

"While the maintenance of children in orphan asylums costs other states from fifty to one hundred dollars per year for each child," Collins wrote, "the large number who are successfully indentured into good homes by the 'Michigan plan' as it is generally known, has reduced the average expense to the state per child from year to year to less than twenty-eight dollars, and the 'Michigan plan' places children in that best of all places for their successful growth to the ideal manhood and womanhood, the homes of its people."

Those who didn't share Collins's rosy view of "placing-out" included Coldwater's superintendant from 1875 to 1883, Lyman Alden. In 1885, he read a paper at the National Conference of Charities and Corrections titled "The Shady Side of the Placing-Out System."

Lyman was an idealist, and judging from his writings, he both hoped for and worked to create the best possible conditions for Coldwater children. In one annual report to the state legislature, he indirectly criticized that body for failing to provide toys. "While no provision has yet been made by the Legislature for the purchase of playthings, such as croquet sets, carts, balls, etc., etc., still the children have managed to extract considerable fun out of pretty scanty material...a base ball club has been organized."

Lyman was also a realist, with a clear-eyed view of the deficits of "placing out" and the integrity to be blunt about it. He began his conference paper, "It is well known by all who have had charge of the binding out of children that the great majority of those who apply for children over nine years old are looking for cheap help." Lyman went on to quote no fewer than seven prominent child welfare officials from around the country who agreed.

"Now, all this does not prove, nor is it intended to prove, that many good homes cannot be found for children, if proper care is taken," Lyman continued. "I know that thousands of such homes have been found, where the children are treated with affectionate consideration."

Many families found a Coldwater child to love and raise to a successful adulthood, as they weathered the normal worries and trials of parenthood along the way. Ida, captured and in Ypsilanti police custody, wasn't as lucky. The police consulted with the Cursons and with Coldwater's Washtenaw

County agent, Mr. Childs. A decision was made. Ida was returned to Coldwater. It's doubtful that she was allowed to keep her doll.

Ida would remain at Coldwater until she was at least eighteen, two years beyond the school's original age limit of sixteen. At that time, she was one of 172 wards, 46 of whom, like Ida, could read and write. In 1910, Ida was the oldest ward at Coldwater.

One hopes that the apparent absence of records for Ida after age eighteen is explained by her "growth to ideal womanhood" of the day: she left the school, married and changed her name. There's at least a good chance that the resourceful gumption of the thirteen-year-old who successfully navigated around Detroit on her own for a few days helped Ida succeed in later years.

One also hopes that Ida enjoyed a happy adulthood, with enough money to now and then buy some beautiful thing of her own that no one would take away.

Name changed due to living descendant.

THE GIRL WHO BURNED

The house at 160 North Washington stood dark on the night of December 7, 1908. The nineteen-year-old servant girl woke up in her attic room at about midnight. She had to go to the bathroom. Though Bertha wore a union suit under her nightgown, the room was chilly.

She got up and sleepily felt for the kerosene lamp on her bedside table. She lifted the glass chimney and lit the lamp. The chimney slipped. Bertha grabbed for it. Her nightgown sleeve caught fire. She jerked back. Her sleeve snagged the lamp. It tumbled and broke on the floor, sending splattered fuel and a column of fire up Bertha's back. As flames roared up her nightgown, Bertha screamed and ran for the stairs.

"The girl ran shrieking, a pillar of fire, to the hall below," reported the December 8, 1908 *Ypsilanti Daily Press*, "where Miss Scovill aroused by her screams overtook her and succeeded with rare presence of mind in wrapping her in a couch throw and extinguished the flames. A physician was summoned and it was found that she was burned from her neck to her feet, the flesh being literally baked on her back, arms, and limbs, although not so severely burned across her chest. The fact that she wore a union suit of heavy underwear made the case more serious as it was almost impossible to remove the garments."

The paper continued: "The unfortunate girl suffered intensely through the night and this morning on the advice of the attending physician she was removed to the Homeopathic Hospital in Ann Arbor where it is said her chances for life are very slight because of the extent of the surface burned over and the depth of the burns."

Bertha Thorn was a farmer's daughter. Born on July 28, 1889, she grew up with eight siblings on her parents' (John and Anna) farm near Willis in Augusta Township. Bertha attended the nearby one-room schoolhouse. Her education stopped there.

In the fall of 1904, she was fifteen years old—of age to enter high school. She never went, nor did 90 percent of the children of her generation. In 1901, only 10 percent of children nationwide attended high school. By 1910, that figure had risen to only 14 percent, with only 3 percent obtaining college degrees. A quarter of the population received fewer than five years of schooling.

Had she gone, Bertha likely would have attended the nearest high school, in Ypsilanti. She would have graduated with the class of '07. None of the Ypsilanti High School yearbooks from 1904 to 1907 included her name in the freshman through senior classes.

In the summer of 1908, Bertha found a job in one of the few professions then open to women. She worked as a servant in the home of Henry Scovill, who owned a large lumberyard on Frog Island that, flooded out, was later moved nearby to Huron and Jarvis.

Mere months after she began working came the fire and the agonizing trip to Ann Arbor for help. Skin grafts in 1908 were done using one of three methods. Zoografting used skin from a "frog, chicken, pig, dog, cat, rabbit, or guinea-pig," wrote Stuart McGuire in his 1908 book *Lectures on Principles of Surgery*. McGuire was surgery professor at Richmond's University College of Medicine (now Virginia Commonwealth University) and later its dean and chair of surgery.

The autograft method used a small section of skin taken from another area on the patient's body. For the immense burn covering Bertha's back, this would have been impossible.

The last method was heterografting, which used skin from fresh cadavers. "They usually grow well and should be employed when they can be secured from a satisfactory source," said McGuire in *Lectures*. "They entail the danger of infecting the patient with syphilis, and other diseases which must be carefully guarded against."

McGuire then reflected on a question that many other surgeons wondered about in his era, a question that reveals the frightening lack of knowledge of surgeons then performing skin grafts. Using language of his day, he wrote, "The question of the necessity of the graft being of the same color as the skin of the patient on which they are planted is still unsettled. It is claimed that a negro's skin grafted on a white person will lose its pigment and that a white skin grafted on a negro will become pigmented."

It seemed almost a cruel joke to predict that Bertha would survive. On April Fool's Day 1909, she was released from the hospital to rest at home. Bertha rode a wagon over washboard dirt roads back to Willis. "She stood the journey very well," reported the April 1, 1909 *Ypsilanti Daily Press.*

The paper continued: "Since she has been in the hospital she has submitted to several skin grafting operations, one being on her right arm. During her illness she has suffered intensely and has been obliged to lie on her face all the time because of the injuries to her back."

On April 11, 1911, Bertha married John Wagner. She had her first child, James, eight months (minus one day) later. The Wagners moved to Milford, where John worked as a farm laborer. Bertha had a son, George, in 1915 and a daughter, Angeline, in 1919. A year later, son Fred was born, with Russell following in 1924, when Bertha was thirty-five. She had one more son, Frank, who did not survive.

The family moved back to Ypsilanti, where John worked for years at the Central Specialty Company, which produced metal parts and plumbing fixtures. The couple bought a house on Holmes Road just northeast of the city.

Bertha outlived her husband. Nearly half a century after Ann Arbor doctors had saved her life, Bertha died on August 9, 1955, at sixty-six years old. She is buried at Union-Udell cemetery.

STORY COMES FULL CIRCUIT

As 1900 began, seventy-seven-year-old York Township farmer Horace Parsons knew that his wife, Maria, was gravely ill. His first wife, Margaret, had died half a century earlier, three years after their New Year's Day wedding. Horace married his second wife, Mary Ann, on New Year's Day

1850. Just months later, his mother, Rebecca, died. The following year, Mary Ann died, possibly in childbirth, and Horace's father, Orrin, died as well. Horace had seen them all laid to rest at Saline's Oakwood Cemetery.

Horace married his third wife, Maria, on May 14, 1860. Over their four decades together, Horace and Maria shared the hardships of nineteenth-century Michigan farm life. They lost one of their children. They survived lean years early in their marriage, selling off sheep, pigs and farm machinery. Unlike some neighbors, they hung on to their mortgage, expanding the farm from thirty acres to fifty in 1870 and sixty-six a decade later.

That year, Horace's restored flock of sheep was up to nearly eighty head and thirty lambs, plus cows and pigs. He grew oats, beans, wheat, potatoes and Indian corn and tended two acres of apple trees. His and Maria's place was the typical mixed-crop, mixed-livestock Washtenaw County farm of the era. The heterogeneity of their farm and those of their neighbors was insurance against the not uncommon disasters that regularly struck down one or another animal or crop.

Now his and Maria's time together, he could see, was ending. Horace had hired a local girl to help. Mabel was a teenager, though neither the term nor the concept existed when she came on as a servant on Horace's farm. Mabel was the oldest child of brickyard worker and general laborer Orson Pepper and his wife, homemaker Myrtie. The young mother had been a schoolgirl only shortly before Mabel's birth in 1884.

Mabel lived in the Parsons farmhouse with Horace, Maria and the couple's two unmarried adult children, Charles and Minnie. In July 1900, Maria died of what was determined to be heart disease. Just three years later, Horace died at age eighty of what was thought to be Bright's disease, a kidney ailment.

By 1905, Mabel had five younger brothers: Bina, Glen, Carl, Thayer and Orville. The family moved to Ypsilanti, settling in a small frame house at 212 Normal Street.

Orson and Glen got jobs as laborers, Bina was hired as a railroad worker and Carl clerked in G.B. Dunlap's Michigan Avenue grocery. In the fall of 1909, Carl married Alice Webster, a onetime house servant of Ypsilanti bank cashier and Peninsular Paper Mill secretary Daniel L. Quirk.

It may have been due to Alice and Carl's connection that Mabel was hired by Quirk. By 1910, she worked as a domestic in the large Quirk mansion on North Huron. Mabel was experienced and a good worker. Known for her cooking, she likely cooked for the Quirks. One dessert specialty of Mabel's still fondly remembered by a living granddaughter is "Blueberry Grunt," a hot blueberry cobbler studded with dumplings and served with cream.

As with her hiring in the Quirk home, the next turn in Mabel's life may also have come from family connections. Her brother Bina worked as a railroad teamster. A fellow railroad employee was called "Lon," short for Alonzo. In the fall of 1915, Mabel married Lon in Potterville in Eaton County. The couple moved to Albion, where Lon worked as a railroad foreman.

Mabel and Lon's respect for family tradition showed in their children's names. Mabel's first child, born in 1916, was named John Orson, a combination of the names of Mabel's and Lon's fathers. Mabel's daughters' names—Myrtie and Olive—honored Mabel's and Lon's mothers. Mabel's son's name—Hugh Alonzo—commemorated the infant's paternal great-grandfather and father. Mabel's fifth and last child, Frieda, was born in 1924.

The family moved to Parma in Jackson County. Money was tight. While many of their neighbors owned the new technology, a radio set, they did not.

In time came a move to a farm in nearby Springport that had belonged to Lon's grandfather and father. The former teen servant now had a family and a home of her own. She also had a car, though according to one living descendant, "I never saw my grandmother drive and do not think she ever learned. Their old car had been around so long and she was so short and heavy that the seat springs on the passenger side were so crushed that she almost literally sat on the floor and could not see [through] the window."

That's the recollection via e-mail of Mabel's grandson, who as a boy visited the Springport farm with his father, Hugh. Now a Saline-area resident, Don still recalls those occasions.

"My vivid memories of overnight stays as a young boy there included sleeping on itchy flannel sheets in a very cold upstairs bedroom," Don remembered, "and trying very hard to not have to go outside to the two-holer outhouse (complete with Sears catalog) until the light of dawn arrived."

The onetime servant girl had become a beloved grandmother. "[She] was very short and very round," wrote Don. "She was known as a good cook and did everything from scratch, including making her own butter, which always had a salty taste to preserve it longer."

After family dinners, the playing cards came out. "The nightly ritual often included playing Canasta," wrote Don. "My grandmother would fall asleep between her plays and my grandfather would yell 'Mabel, wake up god dammit!' to which she would inevitably reply 'I was just resting my eyes' as she scanned the table to try to figure out what cards had been played."

Don described his grandfather Lon as a survivor "who had scratched out a living anyway he could. My father [Hugh] told me that Lon…would make money by taking his team of horses out after a big snow storm and offer to pull stranded cars from the ditches for a dollar, which was a lot of money then." Sometimes they say that family traits skip a generation. It may be that Mabel and Lon's lives of hard work made an impression on their grandson.

Don continued, "[Lon] taught me to play cribbage (I think I was about 11 or 12) by showing me how to count the points for one hand. After that, his 'rule' was that he got to take all the points I missed for himself." He concluded, "It made me a quick learner."

That quick learner excelled in school. He earned a master's, a doctorate and a UM law degree. He worked as a U.S. Army lawyer and later for

Lilly Noble, a domestic at Richard Quayle's home, in August 1903. *Courtesy of Ypsilanti Archives.*

local law firms. Don went on to serve as city councilman and then mayor of Saline. He taught at Thomas Cooley Law School, Oakland University, the University of Maryland and Eastern Michigan University, where he still teaches (he founded an EMU scholarship fund and served as an EMU regent for good measure). He published, among numerous professional articles and chapters in legal publications, a book on the use of forensic science in the courtroom.

Don's even been on NPR twice to discuss the "CSI Effect." This theory posits that TV courtroom dramas' emphasis on seemingly infallible forensic technology has influenced real-life jurors to more readily acquit if the same high-tech evidence doesn't appear in a real court. (Don's verdict: Nope.)

The gentleman who remembers itchy sheets and farmhouse meals of long ago is today the chief circuit judge for Washtenaw County's trial court, the Honorable Donald Shelton.

Just as Mabel honored her ancestors, Judge Shelton and his wife, Marjorie, remember theirs. One prized family possession is a silver napkin ring passed down from Mabel's daughter, Myrtie. In addition, Judge Shelton noted, the extended family still observes "an annual reunion, called the Culver Cousins Reunion after our progenitor Phineas Culver who migrated from upstate New York to Mooreville, Michigan [in York Township] through the [then] newly available Erie Canal…This year we will hold our 99th reunion."

One only wishes that Mabel could also attend, to share some Blueberry Grunt with her grandson and his family. She'd beam with pride.

Part V

THE NEIGHBORHOOD

CARP-OCALYPSE

In 1973, the Michigan Department of Natural Resources wanted to turn Ypsilanti's Ford Lake into a fisherman's paradise. They planned to stock it with muskellunge, rainbow trout and large- and smallmouth bass.

The only problem was the lake's population of "rough fish"—mostly the common carp, plus bullheads and suckers. Carp are not native to Michigan. They were introduced in the late nineteenth century by the era-equivalent of the DNR as a valuable food fish that was cheap to keep in artificial ponds dug on farmers' land. The farmers' aquaculture projects inevitably spilled into Michigan waterways.

A century later, the DNR planned to douse Ford Lake with the piscicide rotenone to kill the carp and other rough fish and then whisk the remains into the Ypsilanti Township landfill and restock the pond. Instead, the project led to a statewide ban on rotenone.

The first step was to lower the lake level. Rotenone was expensive, and a smaller quantity of lake water would mean less poison. Upstream organizations in charge of various sections of the river and its dams agreed to help. The dams were closed, and the level of water in Ford Lake dropped by a yard.

One setback at the beginning of the project presaged the disaster to come. After the rotenone had been delivered and stored on the banks of Ford Lake, someone decided that it would be a hoot to roll the fifty-gallon metal barrels into the water. Scuba divers had to be hired to fish out the barrels.

The local organization overseeing the project was JYRO, the Joint Ypsilanti Recreation Organization. JYRO expected that a thousand or so volunteers on shore and in boats would assist in the cleanup, based on an informal survey of local residents. The organization scheduled the task on Mother's Day weekend. JYRO expected so many private boats to turn out on the lake that the DNR sent down a special marine safety boat to supervise the fleet.

On May 10, the barrels of rotenone were loaded onto a few small motorboats and laid on their sides, two to a boat. Hoses led from the openings in the can lids, running along either side of the boat pilot and extending over the stern into the water churned by the power motor. Sitting a foot or two from one hundred gallons of poison, the pilots were not furnished with protective gear.

Rotenone was harmless to humans, said DNR fish biologist Walt Root, as quoted in the May 9, 1973 *Ypsilanti Press*. "'It's a dehydrating agent,' he explained. 'I had a mouthful of it once as an experiment, and it dries your mouth. Fish are highly allergic to it...[i]t causes the blood vessels to shrink in the gills.'" The paper added, "Labels on the drums, however, indicate the chemical is toxic."

"The boats skimmed gingerly across the lake," stated the May 11, 1973 *Ypsi Press*, "depositing the liquid in their spray." The poison sank into Ford Lake's murky depths. Dead fish began to wash up on shore. The newspaper presented this as a culinary opportunity.

"Anyone who can make it to the banks of Ford Lake," suggested a May 11 *Press* article, "can take home all the fish he can eat for the next few days in the wake of [the fish kill]. The thousands of dead fish, mostly carp, are free for the taking. JYRO officials say they must be carted away and are giving area residents first crack at the kill."

Press food writer Dorothy Zack seized the occasion to publish fish recipes. Her May 15 column, headlined "Lots of Fish Around Gives New Menu Ideas," noted, "The fish kill in the waters of the Huron River and Ford Lake bolstered household stocks of fish for the dinner table...those that went into the freezer are still waiting for new recipes." She advised dipping filets in whipped eggs and coating them in cracker crumbs or cream of wheat. The photo accompanying the article depicted a massive slab of salmon that dwarfs the smaller filets available in supermarkets today. Residents didn't bite.

But "fishing" with rotenone wasn't such a far-fetched idea. Derived from the roots of plants in the pea family, rotenone had been used for years by indigenous people in South America and Australia for fishing. When the plant roots were crushed and thrown into the water, dazed fish would surface for capture and consumption. The use of plants containing rotenone or other poisons for fishing was widespread. Various Native American peoples used black walnut, horse chestnut, poke and other plants. Fishing with poison was practiced in the Pacific Islands, India and Africa—on every continent, in fact.

Rotenone works by absorption into fish gills. Though the World Health Organization classifies rotenone as a "moderately hazardous" poison, and a link to Parkinson's disease has been suggested by clinical trials, generally it is poorly absorbed in the human digestive tract, though it is deadly to fish. Rotenone breaks down quickly in the environment. It's also used as an insecticide and pesticide. The DNR had used rotenone in Michigan since the 1930s.

Nevertheless, the crowds of eager fish harvesters and shore cleaners and the fleet of boats never appeared on Ford Lake. Dead fish continued to accumulate. Then someone in charge of the dam at the south end of Ford Lake opened it by mistake. Poisoned water poured into Belleville Lake. In its morning May 14 edition of the newspaper, the *Press* called it a "mishap." By the evening edition, the story had expanded, and the headline had changed to "Thousands of Fish Killed in Belleville."

The May 14 *Press* quoted DNR fish biologist Ed Bacon, who "said the poisoning was embarrassing…'Dead fish do smell, and sometimes they smell all the way to Lansing.'" His words would prove prophetic.

As the fish continued to pile up on Ford Lake's shoreline, large black flies appeared. Rats were seen, and some were shot with air rifles. The handful of clean-up staff worked desperately to shovel up and bag the fish and heave the bags into a front-loader, but they couldn't keep up. Irate calls were coming in to Gary Owen, a Democratic state representative involved with the cleanup. He authorized a group of 105 state prisoners to transfer from Pontiac to Ford Lake to help pick up fish.

The paper issued an invitation to residents to come down to the now fetid shoreline, mingle with the felons and pick up fish corpses. Invitation declined.

"[JYRO] is mad because too few citizens have come out to help," reported the May 18 *Press*. "JYRO was counting on the help of close to 1,000 volunteers, that estimate drawn from responses received before the planned fish kill. But E.L. Abbott, JYRO chairman, says only about 25 people have come out."

The original estimate of 150 tons of fish carcasses had been surpassed days ago. Dead fish kept coming. In desperation, a makeshift "road" was plowed down one steep lake bank for the front-loader. This road consisted of a section of lakeside scraped bare at an angle so precipitous that in another era it might qualify for its own reality show. The front loader crept carefully up and down the slope, and the tonnage of fish continued to climb.

The community hoped for relief. On May 22, the paper published an article optimistically headlined "Fish Clean-up Almost Finished," though in fact the effort was only a little more than halfway done. Four hundred tons of fish had been removed. The prisoners and clean-up workers had left the project. "But [state fish biologist Walt] Root didn't see that as posing any problem," the article indicated, "as all the remaining fish are on the south side of the lake and away from residential areas."

The following day's *Press* story, headlined "Fish Outlook Good in Two Area Lakes," was even more upbeat. "At Ford Lake, DNR has begun restocking the lake while cleanup of dead fish continues," it noted. "About 92,000 rainbow trout were put into the lake Tuesday and before the week is out DNR plans to stock 100,000 smallmouth bass and 1.75 million walleye fry…in the future, there are plans to stock pure-bred muskies, large mouth bass, hybrid sunfish, and channel catfish. Ed Bacon, DNR fish biologist, said the potential for fishing in Ford Lake was 'terrific.'"

One day later, the DNR issued a statewide ban on rotenone. "The accidental killing of thousands of fish in Belleville Lake has prompted a temporary ban by the Department of Natural Resources on chemical fish kill projects in Michigan's lakes," reported the May 24 *Press*.

The ban didn't last long, however; that fall, the DNR proceeded with a rotenone fish kill in Belleville Lake, as had been planned months earlier. Cooler temperatures alleviated smell problems. The smaller project was completed. The Ford Lake fish kill saga had ended.

A summer walk on the boardwalk in Ford Lake's North Bay Park offers a chance to pause on the bird-watching platform near a reed field and examine the foot-deep lake bottom, rippling in wavy light. Carp-sign consisting of squiggly S's in the sand reveals where carp in the shallows wiggled around in the warm water, looking for delectables.

Carp love canned corn and bread bits. Leftover spaghetti and pieces of old hot dog buns are their foie gras. They even like canned peas, possibly the only organism who does. You may as well bring some nummies to the park next time, in homage to this ineradicable fish. Despite poisons, front-loaders, trucks, state representatives, improvised roads, drained lakes, fish-plucking felons and the efforts of an entire state's Department of Natural Resources over decades, they're not going anywhere.

Fluffy Sparrow Heads

In the late nineteenth century, an interloper was committing thievery across Michigan. Now glimpsed here and there, the miscreant evaded capture, flitting away. Finally, in the late 1880s, the state responded to residents' outrage and levied a bounty on the culprit's head—its tiny, fluffy head. The offender was the English or house sparrow.

"This detestable bird is an imported resident," said Charles Chapman in his 1881 book *History of Washtenaw County*. The English sparrow had been introduced in Brooklyn in 1852 in the hope that it would eat harmful insects. The bird quickly spread across the continent. Today it is the world's most widely distributed wild bird.

Chapman continued: "A few pair first made their appearance here in 1873; the streets of Ann Arbor are now overrun with them, and they are gradually making their way to the country. Wherever they locate they drive out the martin, blue-bird, swallows…They are a seed-eating bird, and in portions of Europe do great damage to the crops of the farmer."

In an early twentieth-century edition of the Michigan Agricultural College's (MSU's) quarterly bulletin, zoological instructor Allen Conger echoed Chapman's disapproval: "The English Sparrow was deliberately introduced into this state in the years 1875–76 by the release of a few pairs of birds at Jackson and Owosso. It is significant to note that just ten years later the Legislature deemed it necessary to pass a bill authorizing bounties on English Sparrows…[T]he state has…attempted by various bounty measures to hold in check this feathered alien."

Conger continued: "Some years ago every attempt at sparrow control met with a storm of indignant protest from well-meaning but misinformed bird protectionists. Today the status of the English Sparrow is so clearly defined that not even the most ardent bird lover will argue against any measure which tends to reduce the numbers of this relentless enemy of native song birds." Conger spoke in defense of "[t]he average citizen, wearied by the Sparrow's incessant chirping and filthy habits."

"Many persons have a strong prejudice against the English sparrow, without knowing why," wrote Michigan Audubon Society secretary and treasurer Jefferson Butler, defending the bird in his 1907 book *The History, Work & Aims of the Michigan Audubon Society.*

Butler continued: "Who can look at this bird with the temperature about the zero mark, hopping through the snow and chirping as happily as though it were a day in June, and say they despise it? They give cheer to many and brighten the lives of the disheartened and the ill, and afford amusement and inspiration to countless children."

One June day in 1889, those children loaded their firearms. "The boys can now depopulate the ornithological part of the county just as rapidly as they choose," offered the August 2, 1889 *Ann Arbor Argus*, "and realize from $1.50 to $3.00 per day [$35.00 to $70.00 today] and thus deplete the county treasury. We append the law, which it will be seen, is explicit in its provisions." It took effect June 16 and provided that:

> [E]*very person, being an inhabitant of this state, who shall kill an English sparrow in any organized township, village or city in this state shall be entitled to receive a bounty of three cents for each sparrow thus killed, to be allowed and paid in the manner hereinafter provided.*
>
> *Every person applying for such bounty shall take such sparrow, or the head thereof, in lots of not less than ten, to the clerk of the township, village or city within which such sparrow shall have been killed, who shall thereupon decide upon such application, and if satisfied of the correctness of such claim, shall issue a certificate stating the amount of bounty to which such applicant is entitled and deliver the same to said applicant, and shall destroy the heads of such sparrows.*
>
> *Such certificate may be presented by the claimant or his agent to the county clerk of the county in which such sparrow or sparrows have been killed, who shall thereupon draw a warrant for the amount on the treasurer of said county, and said treasurer shall, upon presentation of said warrant, pay the same from the general or contingent fund of said county.*

Local boys responded. On August 16, 1889, the *Argus* reported, "City clerk Bach issued the first certificate Monday to Bert Ruthruff for thirty-five sparrows, the bounty amounting to $1.05. Another applicant for bounty killed 108. One Ypsilanti boy is said to have a collection of 900 sparrow heads." This apocryphal boy went unremarked in the contemporaneous *Ypsilanti Commercial*, which unlike the *Argus* did not comment on the ongoing sparrow slaughter.

The *Argus* continued:

> *Over in Saline a large number of orders from surrounding towns are coming in. Deputy Clerk Brown refused to draw any warrants on the treasurer Monday, wishing to wait until the supervisors meet. But the law is imperative in its terms and it looks as if the boys [will] get their money. City clerk Bach will keep a sharp lookout for robins' heads and if any boy is caught killing robins he will be fined $5. Robins and sparrows are two different birds, the one to be fostered and protected, the other to be exterminated.*

Subsequent issues of the paper noted the rising totals of sparrows killed, which climbed to 1,426 by the end of August, though not without incident. "While watching for sparrows last Sunday morning," noted the August 23 *Argus*, "Frank Hoelzle, of Washington Street, shot himself in the foot with his flobert. He is not seriously hurt."

The Flobert was a cheap rifle that shot BBs. The 1902 Sears, Roebuck catalogue advertised the gun, with reservations: "NOTE—WE DO NOT RECOMMEND NOR GUARANTEE FLOBERT RIFLES. Buy a good rifle. It will pay in the end." Caveat or no, Sears sold the Flobert for $1.60 ($40.00 today). Genuine Winchester and Remington rifles in the same catalogue sold for prices ranging from $3.75 to $17.82 ($92.00 to $440.00 today).

As the Floberts fired, Ann Arbor homes suffered damage. The tinkle of broken glass and the danger to passersby prompted the *Argus* to issue a warning on August 30: "The use of firearms in the city is prohibited by ordinance and sparrows within the city limits cannot be shot with them without subjecting the shooter to [a] $5 fine. Marshal Walsh will enforce the ordinance by arresting guilty parties. The enforcement of the ordinance has been made imperative by the carelessness and destructiveness of those who have been using guns. Several persons have narrowly escaped being killed."

The paper continued: "Four dead robins were picked up on State Street one day this week and the tame squirrels were being killed off. One boy shot twenty chippy birds [chipping sparrows]. The boys became so bold that they were going around other people's houses firing at roofs, etc. Many people complain of broken windows."

The sparrow bounty was repealed in 1901 but reinstated a few years later. "The one thousandth sparrow order was issued this morning...County Treasurer Luick has paid out $2,100," noted the August 27, 1907 *Ypsilanti Daily Press.* In subsequent decades, the zest for killing sparrows for meager pennies waned, and the bird became an ordinary member of the local fauna.

However, the sparrow bounty remained valid in Michigan law. A similarly anachronistic law continued to permit Michiganders to break up someone else's logjam in a river in order to facilitate one's own waterborne log transportation. Yet another law mandated that every log placed in a river must bear its owner's log mark, similar to a cattle brand.

Those fearful of the state appearing antiquated due to cobwebbed yet still valid laws can rest assured that Michigan abolished them years ago. Well, a few years, anyways: Michigan governor Jennifer Granholm repealed the log laws, other outdated provisions and the longstanding English sparrow bounty in the year 2000.

SMALLPOX AT EMU

When the 1916 Normal College (EMU) football season was cut short in October, it wasn't due to injuries, lack of funds or academic suspensions. It was smallpox.

The outbreak on campus made news as far away as Connecticut. The November 3, 1916 *Toronto World* noted, "Coach Mitchell and four members of the Ypsilanti Normal College football eleven were stricken with smallpox yesterday...The illness of the athletes was diagnosed last night...Ypsilanti Normal played the University of Detroit last Saturday. Reports from Detroit today said that none of the university's players were ill."

Headlines at home played down the danger. "Smallpox Need Cause No Alarm," read an October 31, 1916 headline in the *Daily Ypsilantian-Press.* The article reported, "That the extent of smallpox in the city is confined to six cases, none of which is severe, and that all possible precautions have been taken to prevent the spread of the disease throughout the city was assured the public today."

The article continued: "Five of the six cases are isolated in the Health Cottage at the Normal, which has been placed at the disposal of the smallpox patients." The Health Cottage was the campus clinic.

Normal College president McKenny called a special assembly of the students, reported the paper. He told them to get vaccinated immediately and show proof of vaccination before leaving for Thanksgiving break. He urged calm. Students expressed "a good deal of indignation," noted the paper, at having to pay for shots.

Many didn't get them. The November 9 *Daily Ypsilantian-Press* reported that three hundred students had yet to be vaccinated and that the number of smallpox cases was rising.

Soon Ann Arborites were being told to stay out of Ypsi, and Normal College students from Ann Arbor were sent home. "Posters enjoining the University [of Michigan] students from making their weekend exodus to Ypsilanti this weekend are being plastered up around the Ann Arbor area," reported the November 14 *Daily Ypsilantian-Press*. UM students would be suspended, said the paper, if they ventured to Ypsi.

By mid-November, the number of cases had risen to twenty-seven. Homes were quarantined. Normal College president McKenny moved out of his own home so that it could be converted into a "detention home for undiagnosed cases of disease," reported the November 14 *Press*. The Health Cottage was full.

The community was afraid: "Complaints stating that occupants in quarantined houses were seen upon the porch were received last week and when questioned today as to how far the quarantine limited the actions of such persons, Dr. Westfall said that their presence upon the porch was well within their rights, but that they should not leave the porch."

Neither quarantines nor smallpox were new to Ypsilanti. In 1882, the city passed "An Ordinance Relative to the Prevention of Small-Pox." Part of it read as follows:

> *It shall be the duty of the keeper of any hotel, tavern, boarding or public house, or the owner or occupant of any private residence, wherein any person may be sick with the small-pox or other infectious disease, to close said public house or private residence, and keep it closed as against all lodgers, customers and persons desiring to visit the same, [until] all danger of communicating the disease from the said house or residence, or from any of the inmates thereof, shall have passed.*

A student-drawn cartoon in EMU's 1917 yearbook found humor in the terrifying disease. *Author's collection.*

The ordinance gave an exception only to doctors and clergymen. When these ministers to the body and soul visited quarantined homes to give hope against death, they risked their own.

The ordinance helped. In 1889, city physician William Pattison gave a report to city council that was printed in the May 17, 1889 *Ypsilanti Commercial.* After noting that there had been twenty-seven cases of scarlet fever that year, Pattison said, "Small pox, which has prevailed more or less over the state, has not appeared in our midst."

Other communities were less fortunate. The February 15, 1889 *Ypsilanti Commercial* reported that in nearby Azalia, Michigan, "the small pox has so far abated that two of the houses will be renovated this week, there being no new cases in the last two weeks."

The *Commercial* that day also urged readers to get vaccinated: "[G]o and have your family physician scratch your arm, apply the little wafer-like, bony point that contains that horrid stuff, that in one week's time with nearly every one that tried it, causes them to say, 'Oh, my arm, don't touch it' and 'I ache so hard and fast in one moment that I hardly know myself.'"

In 1916, the city held its breath. Vaccinations and quarantines began to have a good effect. The crisis slowly passed, and by spring the city was out of danger. However, the experience left an impact on Normal College students.

Their 1917 yearbook, the *Aurora*, mentions the experience. The football page reads, "[Our] game with the University of Detroit was the last game of the season, for the epidemic of smallpox which broke out at the school compelled Coach Mitchell to cancel the better part of the schedule."

In typical college fashion, students made light of the terrifying disease. One entire page of the 1917 *Aurora* yearbook displays a smallpox cartoon, which includes a depiction of a bedridden patient who is cheering, with the legend, "That grand and glorious feelin'—when Doc decides it's only typhoid."

The cartoon also includes a rendering of the Health Cottage, where many students endured the disease. The cottage is shown blazing with light at night, with musical notes and song lyrics streaming from its windows as residents whoop it up.

This seeming flippancy belies the admirable grit and courage summoned by scared students stricken with the disease. After staring death in the eye, and staring it down, the students of 1917, with their cartoon, put thumb to nose and wiggled their fingers.

The Mystery of EMU's Civil War Blood Vials

"Somewhere in the attic of the science building [now Sherzer Hall] on the Normal College campus there should be two bottles, one containing blood-saturated coal cinders and the other containing the remains of whole blood, the first shed in the Civil War."

In the spring of 1951, Mrs. E.H. Lamb brought a yellowed newspaper clipping into the offices of the *Ypsi Daily Press*. She'd found it in a book where her mother had placed it. The clipping contained information so unusual that the *Press* ran a front-page story.

The bottles, the *Press* article reported, were from a Civil War confrontation in Alexandria, Virginia, on May 28, 1861. Shortly after Virginia seceded, Union

Part of the onetime "science museum" in Sherzer Hall consisted of bottled specimens; the blood vials might be among them in this photo. *Courtesy of Ypsilanti Archives.*

troops entered Alexandria, including members of the First Michigan Regiment commanded by Orlando Wilcox and the Eleventh New York Regiment commanded by Colonel Elmer Ellsworth. Ellsworth spotted a large Confederate flag on the roof of Alexandria's Marshall House Inn. He entered the inn and cut down the flag. On his way downstairs, he was shot by James Jackson, the hotel's proprietor—who was himself shot by Corporal Francis Brownell.

The New York and Michigan soldiers there were mindful of the event's historic gravity. They cut up the blood-soaked stair runner and chipped pieces from the stained stairway as souvenirs. Today a piece of the Confederate flag that Ellsworth removed is in the Smithsonian.

"No one on the campus knows how the vials appeared at the college," reported the 1951 *Press* article. The vials were said to contain samples of spilled blood from both Jackson and Ellsworth. "[I]t is assumed that some alumnus or friend, who was a member of the First Michigan Infantry at that time, sent them."

Perhaps it was Brownell himself. After the war, he became a federal pension examiner, whose work involved travel. In November 1885, he visited Ypsilanti. "At the Follett House [a Depot Town hotel] was Francis E. Brownell, who avenged the death of Col. Ellsworth at the Marshall House in Alexandria, Va.," read a November story in the 1885 *Ypsilanti Commercial*, adding that he was here on official business.

Had Brownell donated the blood vials at that time, it seems likely that the *Normal News* student newspaper would have commented on the event. The October 1885–February 1886 issues do not mention the vials. The chatty "Locals" column, however, printed other important news tidbits.

"Gum!" announced the October 1885 issue. "All the rage. Girls can not talk enough, so [they] resort to gum that they may exercise their jaws."

In 1885, the college had a motley collection of bones, preserved specimens, antlers and other bric-a-brac that it called a natural science museum. The December 1885 *Normal News* noted some recent acquisitions to the museum: skeletons of a frog, snake and fish, some corals and shells and a number of prepared bird skins, one from a hawk that measured forty-seven inches from wingtip to wingtip. The paper made no mention of the blood vials.

If not Brownell but rather another member of the Michigan contingent in Alexandria donated the vials, when might that person have done so? One likely time could have been the spring of 1894. Brownell died on March 15, 1894, and the newspaper clipping presented to the *Press* was written on the occasion of his death. The clipping was from an unknown, nonlocal paper, but it may be that the vials were donated in his memory.

Once again the *Normal News* is silent on the subject, though 1894 issues continued to post updates on the ever-expanding museum collection. "Several hundred mosses and liverworts have also been added...Prof. Macoun generously added a package of ferns and lycopods." Other additions included sedges and catkins.

The final place in history in which to rummage around for the blood vials is February 1951, when the *Press* story ran. One would think that the *Normal News* would investigate the story, but the next issue that came out following the *Press* story doesn't mention it. The lead story revealed that celebrated jazz drummer Gene Krupa would perform at the upcoming J-Hop dance. Following issues are also mum.

By 1951, the onetime museum had been forgotten. Upon receiving the old clipping, the *Press* had quizzed Dr. Clarence Loesell, then the director of EMU science programs. Loesell told the *Press* that he had no idea about any such onetime museum. Somewhere in time, the tusks, skulls, shells and liverworts had disappeared, as had, for nearly a century, the name of the vials' donor.

A final search around the most likely date of the old newspaper clipping, Brownell's death in the spring of 1894, finally solved the mystery, in an April 6, 1894 *Ypsilanti Commercial* article: "It was David A. Wise...who sent to the Normal, thirty-three years ago, the bottles containing blood of Col. Ellsworth and his slayer Jackson. He says he scraped up the blood from the floor, after the bodies had been removed, enclosed it in the vials, and sent them to Prof. Welch, the Principal of the Normal. [First Lieutenant] Wise was the first man to enlist in this county." Wise is listed on the first enlistment roll taken in Washtenaw, along with seventy other men from Ypsilanti and nearby communities.

At the time of his enlistment, the Pennsylvania-born Wise was a thirty-five-year-old Ypsilanti deputy sheriff living on the southwest side of town with his wife, Sarah, his six-year-old son, Frank, and his infant daughter, Alice. David and Sarah had married in Ypsilanti on August 8, 1852.

Wise survived the war, mustering out in the spring of 1862. He passed away on February 4, 1899, and is buried in Highland Cemetery.

In 1989, Sherzer Hall suffered a devastating fire that gutted most of the building. EMU did not demolish the building but rather undertook the greater expense of rebuilding the 1903 hall. The restoration was a success. The fate of David Wise's dusty old vials remains a mystery.

WHEN WORK WAS WALKABLE

A tiring job commute is taken for granted today. In 1910 Ypsilanti, commuting for work outside the city was almost unknown. The few exceptions included traveling salesmen, one or two businessmen with interests in other cities and a scattering of factory girls.

Aside from that small number and farmers coming into town from Augusta, Superior and Ypsilanti Townships to sell produce, eggs and dairy items, the city was a largely self-contained unit of local labor. Nearly every working resident commuted to work nearby within town. Most went on foot, with many returning home for lunch (a welcome break in what was then a standard ten-hour workday). The pattern was the norm for everyone from bank presidents to day laborers.

Who were the Ypsilantians of the walk-to-work era? A century ago, fifty-eight-year-old Charles Anderson worked as a janitor in Ypsilanti's First National Bank on the southeast corner of Michigan Avenue and Washington, next door to a tiny sausage factory and a nickelodeon. Anderson, a black man born in Ohio, and Julia, his white wife of thirty years, lived on the northern end of the historically black neighborhood on Ypsilanti's southwest edge. His job was typical of the extremely circumscribed types of menial labor available to the black Ypsilantians of his day. Nevertheless, Charles saved enough money to own his own home and support Julia without her having to work.

Most of Charles's neighbors worked as day laborers, such as his next-door neighbor at 409 Adams, forty-eight-year-old Canadian-born black laborer Manchester Roper. It's likely that both men walked the short distance to their respective jobs each day.

An aerial view of the paper mill long after Quirk's tenure. *Courtesy of Ypsilanti Archives.*

At work in the bank, Charles likely encountered Daniel Quirk Jr., who worked there as a cashier. The son of one of the bank's founders, Daniel came to work from his elegant 1863 Italianate-Colonial-Georgian home at 206 North Huron, a few doors down from his father's 1860 Second Empire mansion, which stands to this day next door to the Ypsilanti Historical Museum.

Daniel also served as secretary and treasurer of the Peninsular Paper Mill at Huron River Drive and Leforge. When Daniel visited the mill, he may have been driven by his coachman, Manchester Roper. By 1910, Manchester had been hired as one of the two servants in Daniel's household, the other being the aforementioned Mabel Pepper.

In 1910, the Peninsular Paper Mill was in operation around the clock. On the north side of the complex stood the vast beater rooms. Here workers shredded rags from an adjacent storage room in a cutter and dumped them into five enormous bleaching vats. Other employees worked in the nearby machine room, the calendar room (the "calendar" was the name of a piece of machinery) or in the basement's carpentry shop and box factory.

In its early days, the mill supplied paper for the *Chicago Tribune. Courtesy of Ypsilanti Archives.*

The mill employed eighteen female and ninety male workers, many of whom walked to work along the train tracks between Depot Town and the factory. One man operating part of the mill machinery was thirty-eight-year-old Henry Dignan. The Michigan-born son of Irish parents, Henry lived with his wife, Katherine, and their six children on Norris Street, near the current-day Corner Brewery.

Norris Street in 1910 was a small working-class neighborhood. Henry's neighbors included thirty-eight-year-old Archie Harrison, a woodworker for the railroad; thirty-four-year-old factory laborer Ralph Le Munyon; Scharf box factory foreman W. Henry de Nike; twenty-two-year-old carpenter Myron Bennett; and fifty-year-old factory worker George Bridgers.

George's sons both held jobs near their home. Twenty-five-year-old son John worked as a fireman in the Cross Street firehouse, and twenty-one-year-old son George walked a few hundred yards each morning to his job as a laborer in the Michigan Ladder Company on Forest Avenue.

Management of the ladder company also lived within walking distance. Vice-President Charles Deist lived on nearby Maple. President Melvin Lewis's home stood at 615 West Forest Avenue, near the Michigan State Normal College. Treasurer Alton Lewis lived near Melvin at 505 Hamilton, and Secretary G.E. Geer boarded at 313 West Cross Street with his widowed mother, Addie.

Farther west on Cross, just past Depot Town, stood the massive Thompson building at Cross and River. Its proprietor, O.E. Thompson, lived until his 1910 death just two houses east, in a home now subdivided into apartments.

South of the Thompson building on River Street lived several men who worked for Detroit, Jackson and Chicago Railway, the interurban and streetcar company. Its vast car barns and powerhouse belched forth plumes of sooty smoke from East Michigan Avenue between the Huron River and River Street.

DJ&C conductors Jay English and Wilbur Gillespie lived with their wives at 215 River. Chief Engineer Ralph Ensign's home was at 231 River. Merton Hudnutt, living with his wife Bertha at 106 River, worked for the company. Three other employees also lived on the street, and section hand Charles McFall, lineman Hubert White and laborers Sidney Case and Floyd Worth lived on adjoining streets.

The interurban's days were numbered. It wouldn't be long before the novelty of "auto barns"—early garages—appearing in the backyards of the well-off in Normal Park would multiply to render obsolete the many small personal stables and carriage houses there.

Today, aside from a fortunate few, Ypsilantians no longer set out en masse each morning to stroll to work within their city.

RIVER STREET'S DIRTY LAUNDRY

Maggie Smith was not looking forward to a forenoon of sewing pleats. She put down her newest customer's summer dress. Downstairs, she offered to get groceries for her landlady Bertha Hudnutt, in whose home Maggie boarded.

Busy at the laundry wringer, Bertha thanked her and gave her fifty cents. Returning home, Maggie walked east over the Michigan Avenue bridge. She looked up at the three big chimneys over the electric interurban car barn just east of the river. Bertha's husband, Merton, worked there as a motorman. The breeze was sending the usual sooty smoke straight in the direction of the Hudnutt home on River Street. Oh, no; not again. Maggie walked faster.

She reached 106 River and went directly to the backyard, hurriedly placing the groceries in the grass. She ran to Bertha, who was frantically pulling damp wash off the line. Maggie coughed as the flakes of soot in the smoky air settled like tiny black snowflakes on the formerly clean laundry.

"Residents living in the vicinity of East Congress and River streets are bitterly complaining," noted the May 10, 1909 *Ypsilanti Daily Press*, "about the dense clouds of smoke which pour from chimneys at the Detroit, Jackson & Chicago railway barns situated on East Congress Street."

The imposing car barns contained a powerhouse with three enormous coal-fired steam boilers that produced the electricity to run the interurban railway. Interurbans made their own juice because municipal electrical systems often had the wrong voltage for the cars. Also, municipal systems were still in their infancy; as late as 1919, the Detroit Edison Company was still running ads in Ypsi papers that began, "If your house is wired…"

The 1909 paper continued: "The company officials pay no heed to the wails of the people living in that neighborhood and no promise of relief in the near future has been given to their protests." One way to solve the problem would be to install "smoke consumers," which redirected the sooty pollution back into the firebox and eliminated much of the mess.

"A smoke consumer would do away with the nuisance but as it is today, the dense clouds of smoke which are emitted from the chimneys now fill the air with such a large amount of soot that it is practically impossible for the people, who are for the most part home owners, to put any washing out in the yards to dry," the *News* continued. "They are compelled to sit indoors during the summer months as the soot falling down covers the white dresses and fills the eyes."

The paper added that nearby residents planned to get up a petition to ask the railway to install the smoke consumers. Those residents likely included the Hudnutt's neighbors on River Street.

At 101 River, twenty-six-year-old Frank Randall operated a salvage wagon to support his twenty-eight-year old wife, Emma. Though, like the Hudnutts, they had a lodger, they had little money; when Frank died about a year later, Emma went to work as a post office clerk.

At 113 River, the retired forty-nine-year-old Sara Coleman lived with her son, Chester, a twenty-one-year-old machinist. Boarding with them was thirty-year-old dry goods sales clerk Minnie Roys.

Forty-year-old interurban conductor Wilber Gillespie lived with his thirty-three-year-old wife, Hattie, at 215 River. Next door lived another railway worker, thirty-three-year-old Denton Glass with his forty-year-old wife, Emma, and daughters, Jennie, Helen and Clara Bell, who also worked as a dry goods clerk downtown.

Preceptress of Ypsilanti High School, the forty-two-year-old longtime instructor Carrie Hardy, lived with her seventy-three-year-old father Henry at 223 River. Her diary, preserved in the Ypsilanti Archives, suggests that she did not tolerate much nonsense; she couldn't have been happy with the pollution.

Whatever action the residents took, it worked. The problem was solved fifteen days later, claimed the May 25, 1909 *Ypsilanti Daily Press*:

> *After several months of investigation, planning, and unremitting labor, Assistant Supervisor Elmer C. Allen of the D.J.&C. railway announces that he has placed smoke consumers in the boilers at the local power house which practically does away with the greatest part of the smoke nuisance which has been the bane of the lives of the residents of River and Congress streets.*
>
> *Mr. Allen has installed three Westinghouse consumers in the three boilers, the principle of the consumers being to actually cause the smoke and soot which ordinarily goes up the chimney, to fall back on the flame and be consumed.*

In each boiler are three quarter-inch jets, from which there is emitted live steam, which so dampens the soot that it becomes too heavy to rise and is thrown back on the bed of the fire.

The system was demonstrated for the *Press* reporter. "Mr. Ensign ordered the jets of steam turned off, and the smoke poured from the chimney above," noted the paper.

After five minutes or so, when the smoke had gained great headway and was pouring out of the chimney in dense clouds, Mr. Ensign ordered the jets opened and within an incredibly short time, the smoke ceased to come from the chimney and nothing but a white vapor was visible.

"It has taken a great sum of money to install these consumers, but we had intended to do so for some time past," declared Mr. Ensign, "when the recent agitation came up and we hurried our plans rather than have any disagreement with the property owners in this vicinity. These consumers are effective and should remedy the nuisance."

The residents were so pleased that many wrote letters of thanks to Mr. Allen, noted the paper. The smoke had disappeared. In twenty more years, the interurbans would as well, displaced by automobiles. The interurban car barns eventually came down. The era of sooty River Street laundry was over.

WOODRUFF SCHOOL DURING THE DEPRESSION

Before the advent of Ypsilanti's bomber plant, on the eve of the Second World War, the tenth year of the Depression had left some Ypsilanti families in desperate straits. Although city charity efforts and federal assistance programs introduced in the mid-1930s by President Roosevelt helped to some degree, many Ypsilanti families still faced hardship in 1939.

One resource that offered some relief was the nursery school program at the onetime Woodruff School. Built in 1901 by the son of onetime educator and newspaper editor Charles Woodruff, the school stood at the northwest corner of Michigan and Park Streets. Woodruff School was a landmark in the Ypsilanti neighborhood once known as Dutchtown, bordered by Babbitt, Grove, South Street and River Street.

A vintage postcard shows the onetime school located on the northwest corner of Michigan and Park. *Courtesy of Ypsilanti Archives.*

Woodruff's nursery school offered a chance for children to spend time in a safe, cheerful environment, eat a good meal and socialize with other kids. The program was run by Gertrude Lamb. Her husband, Charles Lamb, worked in his father John's downtown grocery at 101 West Michigan Avenue, on the southwest side of Michigan Avenue and Huron. Gertrude and Charles likely walked to their respective jobs from their home at 931 Pearl between Summit and Elm.

Gertrude appears to have cared for her students, even making home visits to check on their welfare. In early April 1939, she allowed an *Ypsilanti Daily Press* reporter to tag along on one visit. The resulting April 6, 1939 *Press* story offers a look at the conditions some Ypsilantians faced.

"It is difficult to realize the need of such an institution as the Nursery School here in Ypsi," reads the story. "On the surface there seems to be little dire poverty but a very little investigation will prove this a misapprehension. A trip with Mrs. Charles Lamb, director of the project, into the homes from which the children come shows that in Ypsilanti there are people living in housing and general economic conditions which it would be hard to find surpassed in a large city."

Many Ypsilanti families in that era lived on wages from Roosevelt's Works Progress Administration. The program employed workers to build roads,

Woodruff's manual training class familiarized children with hand tools. The blackboard lists six "Rules for Planing." *Courtesy of Ypsilanti Archives.*

public recreation facilities, airports and other projects. The wages were welcome but not extravagant. Even with the federal work, local families still experienced difficulties.

The *Daily Press* story continued:

> *The average rent that a family living on WPA wages can pay is about $12 a month [$186 in 2010 dollars]…and for that amount it is almost impossible to find good living conditions here. There are many instances of family groups consisting of ten to 12 members living in one or two rooms, often above stores so that children have no place to play except the streets. Others are living in shacks without adequate heating facilities, without proper sanitation and without a means of obtaining fresh water. This latter condition is especially true of a subdivision east of the city just off Ecorse Road where there are a hundred or so people, all of whom must go more than half a mile to a gas station to obtain water which they carry home in pails and which, before the day is over, becomes very stale and unfit to drink.*

In addition to fetching daily household water from a gas station, some families had difficulty finding enough food. City welfare programs offered some resources, and area farmers donated produce that was stored in the "city barn" on Huron in back of the then city hall on North Huron. Even with this generosity, the food supply was limited. Woodruff School helped children by offering meals to its students, seven years before President Truman instituted the school lunch program in 1946.

"There are people in Ypsilanti who are living on an absolute minimum of food, according to welfare authorities—an amount and quality upon which adults are able to subsist but which is not adequate for growing children," reported the *Daily Press* story. "One case in point is that of a tiny child at the nursery school who after eating all she could hold at dinner at school sighed happily and said, 'This is so good. I won't even be hungry when I get home.' Upon questioning she [said] that her father would not allow her anything to eat at home because there were older children who were not in the nursery school and who had to be fed their one meal a day from the family income which would not cover the child in nursery school."

The newspaper went on to describe another little girl's living situation with her mother and two sisters in a tarpaper shack just outside the city limits. Her classmate, a three-year-old boy, noted the paper, lived in "a tumbledown, unpainted two-room shed in the northeast section of town where he exists in absolute poverty with his parents and numerous brothers and sisters, without furniture or bedding, except a few rags."

Another three-year-old had just lost her mother due to illness, reported the *Press*. Her four-year-old companion from an equally grim home situation was one of the favorites of the class. She loved to dress up using the school's box of donated dresses and hats and perform for the other kids.

The *Press* noted, "Among the saddest stories are those of the children living above the stores in the business section of town. One from which one of the nursery school babies comes consists of two rooms reached after a long, hazardous trek up a dirty stairway, through a dark loose-boarded hall past several storerooms." The student living here and his two brothers and baby sisters had few options to play, and the Depression had left the family without even adequate furniture.

"Story after story could be told, for nearly every one of these children playing so contentedly together in their clean, bright basement rooms at

The interior of Woodruff teacher Laverne Ross's classroom in the early 1900s. *Courtesy of Ypsilanti Archives.*

Woodruff School comes from a home environment similar if not worse than those of the cases cited," concluded the paper.

Happier days were to come for most Ypsilanti families. In the meantime, during that April in 1939, Woodruff School and its staff headed by Gertrude Lamb did much to help the children, now grandparents and great-grandparents, who were fortunate enough to be in their care.

PAPER PENNIES

Local currencies are nothing new to either Ypsilanti or Ann Arbor. In addition to nineteenth-century municipal banks, both cities created local currencies about eighty years ago. They weren't created to boost local spending or civic pride. Ypsilanti created its local currency, called scrip, in the fall of 1931 because the city had no other money to pay municipal employees. The currency included paper pennies.

"It was really just an IOU," recalled Paul Ungrodt, in an April 15, 1975 *Ypsilanti Press* article, one of a Great Depression retrospective series.

"[T]here was no money; hardly anyone could afford to pay taxes, so we made do with the scrip." In the summer of 1929, Ungrodt was proud to have secured the prestigious job of Ypsilanti Chamber of Commerce secretary. A few months later, the stock market crashed.

Ypsilanti's slide into the Depression wasn't immediate, but two years after the crash, conditions were grim. Little federal help was available, aside from a few shipments of federal flour and Red Cross cloth. Ypsi Boy Scouts led door-to-door clothing drives. The used clothes were taken to the city welfare office at Michigan Avenue and River Street, "renovated" and then given to the poor.

Church and social groups held canning parties and put up thousands of quarts of food, some for distribution to the poor. One September 1932 *Ypsilanti Daily Press* article reported that Lincoln schoolgirls in the seventh, eighth and ninth grades canned peaches, tomatoes and pepper relish for winter use in their own cafeteria. The girls also put up sixty-five quarts of concentrated grape juice, made from grapes grown by boys in the school's "agriculture department."

In 1931, one city council member proposed that municipal employees in the "streets and parks departments should be put on a four day shift after Oct. 1," reported a September 22 *Daily Press* article, "and unemployed men put to work under them in shifts to keep the work done and provide labor for those whom the city must help. These unemployed will be paid in scrip which can be used for specified groceries in any city store."

To get the streets and parks jobs, the unemployed had to apply for an identification card. Aside from standard questions about age and address, the applicant had to provide the name and address of their previous employer, whether they were in debt on their furniture, car or anything else and whether they had received any other aid in the past.

The city received four hundred applications. Roughly three-quarters were married men, about half were over forty and about half were white. Fewer than half owned a home but instead rented an apartment, lived in a boardinghouse or rented a single room. Almost one-third of applicants were the sole supporters of their family, and almost one-quarter had more than two dependents. Two women applied.

The number indicated a want that was more pressing than some had believed to be the case. "It should be understood," Paul Ungrodt was quoted in an October 30, 1931 *Daily Press* article, "that many of these unemployed who have registered, although the total is apparently great, are not hard

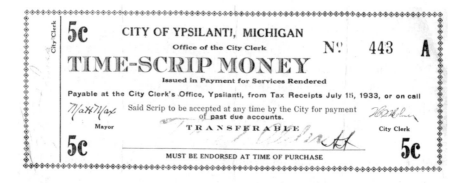

This Depression-era paper nickel was designed and printed in Ypsilanti. *Courtesy of Ypsilanti Archives.*

pressed. Many have relatives and the condition of many others is not serious because they have had work until recently. Furthermore, there are numerous instances where more than one in a family registered."

As a representative of the city's economic health, Ungrodt may have felt a need to downplay the problem. Years later, in the 1975 *Press* retrospective article, he characterized the times more negatively. "If your business failed either you were lucky enough to find someone else to work for or you simply did nothing," he said. "But there weren't jobs for most people. It wasn't a pretty picture by any means."

In preparation for the work program, city officials decided that "the city will profit more and the poor as much by a program of work which will be of permanent benefit rather than the creation of odd jobs of no lasting value," according to an October 10, 1931 *Daily Press* article. City officials planned a 390-foot sewer as the first project, to be followed by work whose cost in scrip and materials could be covered by bonds issued by the city. City clerk Harvey Holmes designed the scrip, and it was printed in town. The article concluded, "'[A]ll who expect dole from the city will be required to give work in return,' Mayor Matthew Max has insisted."

Later that month, the October 21, 1931 *Daily Press* reported:

> *The first issue of scrip money by the city of Ypsilanti was made, when City Clerk Harvey Holmes paid seven men a total of $89.25* [$1,250.00 today, or an average of $180.00 each].
>
> *Scrip will be accepted only for the articles printed on the back of the money, and each piece must be signed by the man presenting it. If he cannot*

write, the merchant accepting the scrip signs for him, and his thumb print is made on the scrip. There will be no change made in either cash or scrip. Persons using it must purchase the full amount they present.

Scrip is issued in denominations of 1 cent, 5 cents, 10 cents, 25 cents, or $1.

The list of items scrip could buy was restricted, the article noted, to "coal, coke [fuel], bread, navy beans, bacon, baking powder, corn meal, corn starch, canned soup, canned peas, canned tomatoes, canned hominy, canned corn, coffee, crackers, flour, lard, matches, milk, macaroni, oleo, oatmeal, onions, potatoes, pepper, prunes, pancake flour, rice, soap, sugar, salt, [baking] soda, salt pork, tea, and yeast." Fresh meat and fish, butter, eggs, cheese and fresh fruits and vegetables were not allowed.

A year and a half later, President Franklin D. Roosevelt passed the Federal Emergency Relief Act, which granted money to the poor. FERA was followed by other New Deal programs that addressed unemployment. Ypsilanti scrip was phased out.

Today, the surviving examples are only a reminder of the onetime local currency, earned with a pick and shovel, that put food on Ypsilanti tables.

Professor of Penmanship

"I have no idea what this prescription says." "Is this an 'm' or an 'n'? Or an 'r'?" "I can't read my own writing."

Birthday cards, checks and grocery lists are today's last refuges of handwriting. In an era of texting, e-mail and keyboards, there isn't much opportunity to practice writing by hand. But there was a time in Ypsilanti when a graceful script was seen as essential to a successful business career. Good handwriting was perceived not only as vital to legible bookkeeping but also as a general signifier of a good education and even personal refinement.

With this in mind, in 1883 Irish immigrant Patrick Roger Cleary opened a school of penmanship in downtown Ypsilanti. Patrick Roger preferred the moniker of "P.R.," given some anti-Irish sentiment of the times. After graduation from Valparaiso University, Cleary circulated around Michigan as an itinerant penmanship teacher. Ypsilanti's Normal College (EMU) attracted him as a possible place to teach, and Cleary settled in Ypsilanti.

LEARN TO WRITE!

P. R. CLEARY, The Well Known Penman and Teacher, will open a School of Penmanship, in the

HALL OVER SHERWODD'S BOOT & SHOE STORE, Ypsilanti,

Cor. Congress & Huron Sts., 2nd Floor.

MONDAY, Oct. **8**, 1883.

This will be a Permanent School.

25 Per Cent Discount

In All Tuition the First Week. For Circulars giving Full particulars, call at School or address

P. R. CLEARY, Ypsilanti, Mich.

Cleary's inaugural ad offered samples of his own Spencerian handwriting. *Author's collection.*

Cleary tacked up specimens of his beautiful handwriting in the downtown post office and placed ads in the local papers, which obliged by running mini-editorials, such as the one in the October 6, 1883 *Ypsilanti Commercial*: "How many need to learn to write. Bad writing a general fault. A successful teacher in penmanship Mr. P.R. Cleary, opens a school over Sherwood's store next Monday evening. Begin with him and stick to it until you become a good writer. Notice fine specimens of penmanship hanging in the post office."

Cleary ran a large ad in the same edition of the *Commercial* displaying examples of his lovely script. "LEARN TO WRITE!" it proclaimed, advertising Cleary's fledgling store at Michigan Avenue and Huron, over a shoe store. "This will be a permanent school," the ad declared. Two students signed up.

The fashionable handwriting style of the day was Spencerian script. The ornamented script had originated in 1848 as a creation of Platt Rogers Spencer. Spencer's sons carried on his work and published *The Spencerian Key to Practical Penmanship* just after the Civil War. Spencerian handwriting remained in vogue until the 1890s, when it was eclipsed by the simplified, speedier Palmer Method.

"Mr. Cleary's writing school is a great success from the start," noted the October 13, 1883 *Ypsilanti Commercial*. "Such a school was much needed."

By October 20, enrollment had grown to fifty-three students, and Cleary had to relocate to larger quarters. He moved his school into the "Union Block," remembered by local old-timers as the "Kresge Block" at 200–212 West Michigan Avenue. Cleary began planning to expand his penmanship school into a larger business college.

Near the end of October, Cleary ran another ad in the *Commercial*: "[Cleary's School of Penmanship] now offers Superior Advantages to Gentlemen and Ladies who are desirous of acquiring a rapid, graceful style of writing, either for business advantages or for successfully teaching

Cleary College stood on the southeast corner of Michigan Avenue and Adams, where EMU's College of Business stands today. *Courtesy of Ypsilanti Archives.*

Spencerian and Ornamental Penmanship. Some of his pupils have already attained a degree of proficiency that would do credit to many teachers of Chirography [handwriting]." Enrollment had swelled to eighty students by mid-November.

Within a year, P.R. Cleary had expanded his School of Penmanship into the Business College. An October 11, 1884 ad in the *Commercial* noted, "FIVE DEPARTMENTS—*Commercial*, English, Penmanship, Short-Hand, and Type-Writing...over 300 enrolled the past year." The school was still housed in the Union Block but would soon move to its own building.

"In 1886, he purchased the property on which the college now stands [at 300 West Michigan Avenue, now the site of the EMU College of Business]," noted Harvey Colburn in his book *The Story of Ypsilanti*. "[I]n the fall of 1887, work was begun on the building...in the fall of 1889, the main structure was finished and dedicated." Cleary Business College had become a downtown institution.

A year earlier, the college celebrated its fifth anniversary, complete with a visit from then governor of Michigan Cyrus Luce, a parade, music, speeches and a banquet produced by the Ladies Aid Society of the Episcopal Church. The event was covered in the October 26, 1888 *Ypsilanti Commercial*:

> *Five years ago Prof. P.R. Cleary came here, and announced through the public print and otherwise that he would open a business college and school of penmanship in the not particularly large room over Sherwood's shoe store. Then, as ever, false prophets abounded in the land, and they took no pains to conceal their belief that in a few short weeks this "business college" would be a thing of the past...But despite this unanimous belief in its failure, the writing class started out well, and the Professor's ability in his particular branches impressed itself upon the students, and they recommended his school to others...from that time until this, though Prof. Cleary has been backed by nothing but ability and "clear grit," the institution has experienced a steady and continuous growth.*

Cleary University has survived to the present day, though penmanship is no longer among its course offerings. It is a business college, with campuses on Plymouth Road in Ann Arbor and in Howell, Michigan. On its website, Cleary president Tom Sullivan notes, "I am especially proud to be affiliated with Cleary University, an institution committed to teaching the American free market economic system, ethical business practices, and leadership skills. Our alumni include small business owners, Fortune 500 executives, mid- and senior-level managers—all solid performers who contribute each day to the promise of America."

Mighty impressive. But one wonders, concerning those eminent Fortune 500 executives: how's their handwriting?

LITTLE NEMO IN YPSILANTI

Ypsilanti's Cleary Business College prided itself on innovative teaching methods. Instead of using textbooks, the school had students practice with such typical business forms as invoices, receipts, checkbooks, insurance policies and mortgages. Students also had a mock bank account with which to set up their own "business" within the school building.

One interior view of the school shows a long hall with booth-like cubicles lining the walls, housing student "businesses." These are labeled "Transportation Co.," "Post Office" and "Commission Co.—Bookkeeping—Cashier." As students mastered the facets of each business, they were sent to another. Cleary taught shorthand, typewriting and business ethics in addition to the hands-on business skills.

To this industrious hive in 1886 came the dreamy young artist Zenas Winsor McCay. Born in Canada in 1867, Zenas was the oldest son of Robert and Jeanette. Soon after his birth, the family moved to Spring Lake village in Michigan's Ottawa County near Muskegon.

The 1870 census lists twenty-eight-year-old Robert as a teamster, twenty-eight-year-old Jeanette as a homemaker, Zenas as three and younger brother Arthur as two. The 1880 census lists Robert as a grocer with three children: twelve-year-old Zenas, ten-year-old Arthur and four-year-old Mary. Robert also worked in a lumber mill.

Zenas, who later called himself Winsor, loved to draw since childhood. His father had a more practical career in mind. In 1886, Winsor and three friends came to Ypsilanti to attend the Cleary Business College. The friends rented a large room together. Ypsilanti was bigger and more bustling than Spring Lake.

However, according to one 1880s Cleary advertisement, "The innumerable attractions of city life which alienate the attention of students from their studies are not to be found in Ypsilanti."

But Detroit had one such attraction: Sackett and Wiggin's Wonderland, a dime museum. Created by P.T. Barnum in 1841, dime museums were a sort of walk-through version of the Victorian "cabinet of curiosities." The museum's ostensible purpose, according to Barnum, was education and moral improvement through entertainment. Dime museums presented a heterogeneous mix of freak shows, circus performances, religious tableaux and sometimes less savory displays—for personal edification. Winsor loved drawing the varied scenes in the dime museum and eventually became one of the attractions, working there as a caricature artist.

In 1888, Winsor displayed a drawing in downtown Ypsilanti. "The work of Art exhibited at the Post Office by Winsor McCay," noted the February 10, 1888 *Ypsilanti Commercial*, "is a great credit to the young man's artistic ability." Later that year, he drew portraits at the annual city fair. "One of the most interesting features, if not the most, that attracts attention on the Fair Ground," reported the September 21, 1888 *Commercial*, "is the portrait drawing by our friend, Winsor McCay, in Agricultural Hall. The crowd that assembles around this young artist is enormous. The portraits are life size, and are completed in the remarkably short time of two minutes."

That ability caught the eye of Normal School geography and drawing professor John Goodison, who had entered the Normal School in 1856 and taught there until his death in 1892. An "In Memorium" in the 1893 Normal School yearbook singles out his patience, perseverance and intelligence—when he wanted to read a geography text written in German, he taught himself German.

When Goodison recognized the talent in McCay's work, he met with and praised the young artist. Goodison had worked in stained glass before teaching at the Normal, and one source says McCay developed his vivid palette in part from the influence of Goodison's stained glass. Less uncertain is that Goodison imparted a strong sense of the power of perspective in art to McCay, whose later *Little Nemo* comic strip is noted for unusual, sometimes breathtaking, perspectives.

Goodison encouraged McCay. In 1889, McCay left Cleary Business College for Chicago and found work drawing advertising posters for a circus. He moved to Cincinnati, married and then moved to New York. In 1904, his comic strip *Dreams of the Rarebit Fiend* began in New York's *Evening Telegram*. The strip presented a series of gradually more surreal events. The last panel always shows someone waking in bed from a dream, regretful for having eaten some odd food, usually rarebit.

Despite the ever-happy ending, elements of some of the scenes recall the charged surrealism and menace (or even terror) in the sometimes psychedelic prints of German symbolist artist Max Klinger. Klinger's famous 1881 series of prints *Paraphrases about the Finding of a Glove*, based on dream images, was widely published and likely known to McCay.

McCay's next comic strip also explored the theme of dreams. In 1905, *Little Nemo in Slumberland* began in the *New York Herald* and ran until 1914, then again from 1924 to 1927. In 1911, McCay made an animated short based on the strip.

The strip has had lasting appeal. In 1989, a group of animators made a feature film based on the strip, *Little Nemo: Adventures in Slumberland*. A 1990 video game, *Little Nemo: Dream Master*, was based on the film. McCay's strip has inspired theatrical productions and has influenced such modern work as Neil Gaiman's *Sandman* graphic novels and Maurice Sendak's book *The Night Kitchen*.

In 1914, McCay created the silent animated short *Gertie the Dinosaur*. He and an assistant made it using thousands of drawings on sheets of rice paper.

McCay presented the cartoon in vaudeville shows and gave Gertie spoken "commands" that she magically "obeyed" on the screen. At the end, McCay walked behind the screen just as a life-sized version of himself appeared on the screen in animated form and went for a ride on Gertie's back.

For many Americans, this was the first cartoon they'd seen, and the effect was galvanic. However, *Gertie* was not the first animated movie. The inventor of the animated movie, according to John Grant's *Masters of Animation*, is generally regarded as J. Stuart Blackton for his 1906 film *Humorous Phases of Funny Faces* or perhaps even Arthur Melbourne for his 1899 *Matches: An Appeal*.

However, McCay was one of animation's pioneers, and his wildly phantasmagoric imagination and elegant, vivid mastery of illustration—nurtured by an Ypsilanti teacher—secured him a lasting place in animation and comic strip history.

Part VI

LEAVING HOME

A PATH LESS TRAVELED BY

In the early 1800s, thick forest covered much of the land south of Ypsilanti.
    The virgin forest nourished huge flocks of passenger pigeons on migratory routes passing north. Often they passed low enough to be knocked from the air with sticks. After one such harvest, according to one Ypsilanti city history, "at dinner that day, there was a tremendous pigeon pot pie, sufficient to satisfy everybody, although there were twenty at the table." But the forest also held danger. One large swamp in Augusta Township was named Big Bear Swamp, and wolves and panthers roamed our county.
    Into this wilderness in 1828 came Andrew Muir with his family. They had fled an economic recession and spiking farm rents in Scotland and immigrated with other relatives to America. Members of the McDougall family also made the trip. After the weeks-long Atlantic crossing, twenty-six-year-old Mary Muir and twenty-nine-year-old George McDougall married in Rochester, New York, on Halloween in 1828.
    The families traveled by boat and overland to Michigan. Andrew Muir bought a small farm near the intersection of modern-day Stony Creek and Bemis Roads, about six miles south of Ypsilanti. He invited his daughter, Mary, and son-in-law, George, to share the property. However, George, who had worked as a miller back home in Ayrshire, chose to settle just south of the small Ypsi settlement and work at its flour mill there.
    Mary often walked down to her father's farm late in the week to see her parents and stay overnight. On Sundays, George would travel down to visit, and he and Mary would return to their home.

One winter day, Mary prepared to visit her parents. She set the table for her husband and made sure that his dinner was ready for his return from the flour mill. Mary adjusted her pretty new calfskin shoes, tied her plaid wool scarf over her dress and left the house. She set off on the faint Indian trail that wound through the six miles of forest to her parents' farm.

The days were getting shorter, and it was shady under the trees, but Mary knew that she could reach her parents' home before nightfall. Snow covered the forest floor, blanketing fallen logs and the crunchy layer of leaves.

In the distance, Mary saw it: an enormous fallen tree blocking the path. There was no climbing over it; she had to go off the path to find a way around. The fallen tree trunk extended far into the surrounding trees. Mary picked her way to its end, working her way around. The afternoon light was fading. On the other side, Mary searched for the path. Then she set off again.

Mary walked on. This was odd; it was twilight and she should have been at her father's farm. And the path looked strange. It dawned on her that at the fallen tree she'd stumbled on a different path, one that was leading her into the wilderness.

Night was coming on. Mary guessed that she must be close to her father's farm and decided to leave the path. She picked her way through the forest. Under the dark treetops, the snow glowed a soft white.

Some time later, Mary knew that she was lost. She decided to return north to Ypsilanti and safety. Mary looked up through the bare branches and found the Pole star. Mary pushed away branches and stepped over logs. The temperature was dropping. She glanced up at the star. Mary tripped and fell, scraping her shoe. She ran a finger over the side of her shoe and felt a rip where the stitching had split.

Mary was exhausted. She decided that she would see better next morning. There was no help for it but to try and rest. She found a nook between a log and a tree trunk and sat down. She unfolded her shawl and draped it over herself, curling up on the frozen ground. Exhaustion overtook her.

Mary's eyes flew open and she sat up. Then she heard it again: a distant wolf howl. Silence. There it was again…and another. A third. Should she run? She might fall again in the dark. Better to stay. Perhaps they didn't know she was here. Was it near morning? Mary took out her husband's watch and tried to read it. She hadn't taken the key to wind it, and it had stopped at one o'clock.

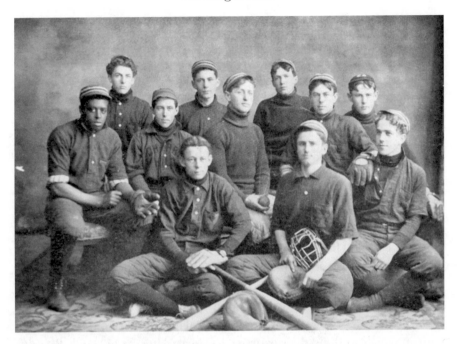

A pioneer in a different sense, Henry Harrison was one of Ypsilanti High School's first black graduates. He was voted into and served as secretary of his 1903 senior class. *Author's collection.*

Hours later, she saw a faint dawn light. She got up stiffly and began walking. The sun passed overhead. The rip in her shoe had widened, and the front sole slapped as she walked. The insole on the other shoe was fraying, letting in snow. It was late afternoon.

Mary heard a dog bark. She altered her course toward the sound. Suddenly, she came upon two cows in a clearing. Mary nearly collapsed with relief. She couldn't see their farmhouse and couldn't go any farther. But the cows would return home for milking time. Mary propped herself against a tree, facing the cows. She dozed. When she awoke, they were gone.

Mary jumped up and looked around. She heard a twig crunch and ran a few steps. She saw the flick of a cow's tail among the twilight trees. Mary ran after it.

At the farmhouse three miles south of Saline and fifteen crow-miles from Ypsi, the farmers welcomed Mary. They fed her, tended to her feet and put her to bed. They told her that if she had walked in a slightly different direction, she'd have been nowhere near a settled piece of land. The next day, they drove her in their wagon back to Ypsilanti.

TWO WORLDS

Eighteen-year-old George Moore boarded the eastbound train on a chilly November day in 1898. Several of his schoolmates climbed on as well. The boys sat near Mrs. Lizzie McDonald, their guardian.

It would be a long journey. Four days and three nights over the clacketing steel rails lay between his Idaho birthplace and a Pennsylvania boarding school.

Built in 1879, the Carlisle School was led by its founder Richard Henry Pratt, a former Civil War volunteer who, after the war, served as an officer in the Tenth Cavalry. Its members included Buffalo Soldiers and Native American scouts. In western Indian Territory, Pratt's group was in charge of enforcing reservation borders to protect settlers' lands; Indians left the reservation to seek food.

Pratt was also put in charge of a group of Native American prisoners; he treated them humanely, comparatively speaking, even giving them sketch pads in which to draw their experiences. Years later, in his book *Battlefield and Classroom*, Pratt wrote, "Talking with the Indians, I learned that most had received English education in home schools conducted by their tribal government. Their intelligence, civilization, and common sense was a revelation because I had concluded that as an Army officer I was there to deal with atrocious aborigines."

However, in his later role as schoolmaster, he also said, "In Indian civilization I am a Baptist, because I believe in immersing the Indians in our civilization and when we get them under holding them there until they are thoroughly soaked." Pratt had firm beliefs about how and why to educate his Carlisle students. In his era, Pratt's assimilationist ideas were progressive.

George Moore, who had taken the train and attended the Carlisle School, eventually returned partway back west—to Ypsilanti.

Pennsylvania: Carlisle School

Carlisle's main building was an abandoned, tumble-down army barracks. The year it opened, students spent much of their time cleaning and repairing the buildings. The curriculum consisted of industrial arts training for the boys, domestic arts training for the girls, academic classes and language classes; not all of the students could speak English. It was the nation's first off-reservation boarding school. One scholar called Carlisle "the flagship of the American Assimilation Era's education program."

George Moore arrived at Carlisle on November 21, 1898, and was placed in a boys' dormitory. George was a full-blooded Nez Perce. The other students came from the Lakota, Oneida, Pueblo, Menominee, Shoshone and numerous other Native American nations. The nation with the greatest number of representative students was the Iroquois, and Klamath, the fewest.

George could already read, write and speak English. He'd previously studied at the Chemawa Indian School in Salem, Oregon. "George Moore" was not his real name, but likely the English name Chemawa had given him, as the school's first enforced step to assimilation.

At Carlisle, the process of assimilation was enforced without accommodating the students' diverse customs, beliefs and cultures. As one small example, male students who had not previously attended a school such as Chemawa received haircuts upon arrival. This act deeply distressed those students for whom hair was cut only when a relative died.

Carlisle taught students ranging from grade school to high school age. George was placed at the high school freshman level. He made it to sophomore year and, in addition to his academic subjects and industrial arts classes, began to learn how to play the oboe. The May 5, 1899 *Indian Helper* school newspaper noted of one concert, "Thomas Morgan and Ralph King gave Saxophone solos, in a manner that pleased all, and Geo. Moore who plays the Oboe, made some merriment with tones on his new and peculiar instrument."

As a junior, George attended two summer "outings." Carlisle's "Outing" program consisted of placing students in local homes to work and become more Americanized. The school deposited their earnings, however meager, in individual student accounts. George worked for a week in early June in Rushland, Pennsylvania, and then switched for a two-month stint in Langhorne.

George was slated for a five-year program at Carlisle and was scheduled to graduate in late spring of 1902. He did not graduate. Most Carlisle students did not; historians estimate that only about one in eight students did.

Ypsilanti: Normal College News

However, by October, George was a student at Ypsilanti's State Normal School, taking a business course. He occasionally may have read the school's newspaper.

At about this time, the *Normal College News* ran an article written by Normal alum and former Ingham County resident Mary Fanson Lawrence. Mary graduated in 1887 and taught Latin and German in Aurelius, a town just south of Lansing. She married Glen Lawrence, and the two traveled west to a small day school at the base of one of the three mesas in the Moqui (Hopi) Reservation in Arizona. Glen taught a class of about forty-five Hopis per day in Polacca school.

Though some women worked at two larger schools elsewhere on the reservation, Mary worked as a housekeeper. In 1901, Glen earned $72 a month ($1,830 today), and she earned $30 ($763). Their combined salaries had the modern-day value of $31,000 per year. Mary composed an essay about her life in Arizona, "Life Among the Indians of the Southwest." She sent it to her alma mater.

"Friends have written, 'In what part of Arizona is your town? We cannot find it on any map!'" reported her May 28, 1904 *Normal College News* article.

The traveler leaves the Santa Fe R.R. for the Moki Reservation…the villages are from 65 to 75 miles north, and about 100 miles from the Utah line. The journey takes one across the Painted Desert and seemingly endless stretches of sand, past great buttes, and around or over mesas, until the weary traveler is awed by the vastness of the desert.

The towns are seven in number, three of the villages being built upon an almost perpendicular rocky mesa, 6000 feet above the plain. It is known as the First Mesa…The villages were built on the high mesas so the Hopi could protect themselves when attacked by the Navajos. The houses are built side by side, like modern flats, of stone; and are from one to three stories high, built in terrace fashion, and entered by ladders on the outside; the roof of one room on the ground will be the front steps or yards of the next story, and so on. The rooms are low and we have to stoop to get around in them. The streets are narrow alleys, and the tourist has to pick his way among burros, chickens, dogs, and turkeys.

Mary went on to say that some of the students had never attended school. "Of course, as they do not know a word of English when they enter school, and in looks and attainments are mere animals, the progress is necessarily very slow. When a child comes to us we give it an English name, as life is too short to spend in learning and pronouncing such names as Tuvayhongeva, Inowanghoeonsa, or Musaquaptewa."

The curriculum included Christian instruction. "At Christmas time," said Mary, "one of our large boys was helping to carry some pies which were being made for their dinner. He began singing, 'In the Sweet Pie and Pie,' entirely unconscious of any parody."

Mary's essay did not describe the Hopi perspective or belief system. It described such outward appearances as clothing styles and marriage customs. She likely did not know that the reservation's village of Oraibi was and is one of the oldest continuously occupied settlements on the North American continent, founded before the year 1100.

Mary expressed irritation with other nonnative visitors who disagreed with the school's mission. "There are many interesting things about these people, and they are visited frequently by sight-seers, ethnologists, and tourists, who are often a hindrance to us in our work, because they want this region to remain a show ground for the future, and talk or use their influence against any change or progress."

Mary concluded her essay with the remark, "The Hopis are good-natured, light-hearted children, easily led in the wrong way by presents of candy and tobacco. Like children they need disciplining, and do not always regard those whose duty it is as their best friends."

Coda

The fate of George Moore after his study in Ypsilanti is unknown to the writer. According to Barbara Landis, the Carlisle Indian School biographer for the Cumberland County Historical Society, a note in his onetime school file says that he died sometime before 1918, in his late thirties.

Mary Lawrence died in 1935 at about seventy-two. She and Glen are buried at Maple Grove Cemetery in Ingham County.

On the Hopi reservation, Polacca Day School, the onetime home of Normal graduate Mary Lawrence and her husband Glen, was replaced in 2004 by a new K–6 elementary named First Mesa Elementary School.

The $20 million project, funded mostly with monies from the Bureau of Indian Affairs, was managed by the Hopi tribe. The building was designed to reflect Hopi culture. Plans were drawn by Dyron Murphy Architects, a Native American–owned architectural firm.

Natural light fills the school, plumbing is superefficient, no potable water is used for the xeriscaped grounds' drip-irrigation system and the structure is designed to minimize heat absorption. The school reflects Hopi culture and ecological values, which survived the age of assimilation, in a high-tech, modern manner. First Mesa Elementary is the first LEED-certified school in Arizona.

THE BIRCH-BARK TIPI

Few Ypsilantians are neutral on the subject of the onetime EMU Huron logo. Some regard the green Native American profile as exploitative and others as an homage to former area Native Americans. A less ambiguous homage to a different group of former local Native Americans was made one hundred years ago when EMU erected a birch-bark tipi in a prominent spot on campus.

In its last issue before summer break, the *Normal College News* previewed the event, calling the structure a 'wigwam.' "In the dedicatory ceremonies, will be given a history of the wigwam…The events will be made a city affair, the city officials and the heads of the schools being present."

The event made the city news as well. The June 14, 1911 *Ypsilanti Daily News* read, "The Indian tipi, which has been bought by the advanced nature study class…is to be erected on the Normal campus east of the Science building [today called Sherzer Hall]."

The tipi had belonged to Native American activist and writer and Potawatomi chief Simon Pokagon. Pokagon built the tipi in his home of Hartford in southwestern Michigan for display at the 1893 Chicago World's Fair. Pokagon had noted the absence of Native American representation at the fair and asked Chicago mayor Carter Harrison if he could attend. Harrison welcomed him and sent travel expenses, and Pokagon and his tipi traveled to Chicago. While he was there, Pokagon gave a speech informing the audience that his father, Leopold Pokagon, had once owned the land on which Chicago had been built.

The tipi stood on the eastern side of what is now called EMU's Sherzer Hall. *Courtesy of Ypsilanti Archives.*

After its term at the World's Fair, the tipi was exhibited in various sites around the country. Measuring twenty-four feet high and sixteen feet in diameter, the structure consisted of horizontal concentric rings of a double layer of white birch-bark attached to tipi poles, with a small doorway.

After Pokagon's death in Hartford in 1899, the tipi was erected in the yard of C.H. Engle, a lawyer who had assisted the Pokagon band of Potawatomis for many years in its struggle for reparations. When Engle indicated his willingness to sell the tipi, EMU students held a sale to raise money for its purchase. Engle attended the dedication ceremonies on June 16, 1911.

Another guest at the ceremonies was Pokagon's granddaughter, Julia Pokagon, who attended the ceremony in traditional dress, wearing a long decorated skin tunic and a headdress of feathers. She was accompanied by her husband, Quakomo, who also wore traditional dress. After introductory remarks by EMU professor William Sherzer, head of the Natural Sciences Department, Julia spoke.

According to the June 16, 1911 *Ypsilanti Daily Press*, she said, "I am glad that I am here: indeed glad that you have granted a child of the forest an opportunity to address teachers and students of the grandest institution in Michigan. I am glad this college has honored my race by placing on these grounds the wigwam of my [grand]father."

Julia went on to recount the painful history of the forced Potawatomi removal from the Great Lakes region, as well as the story of those who managed to remain in Michigan. She said, "[M]y heart is joyous as I contemplate the fact that the Pokagon band escaped banishment and fled to this state. They were kindly received with open arms. Michigan was at that time was less than one year old [in 1837]."

She continued, "[Indiana] demanded of infant Michigan that we should be given up and exiled with the rest of the Potawatomi tribe. All praise to young Michigan! She boldly declared to her sister state, 'Stand back! You shall not molest a single child of the forest within all our borders,' and within a few years thereafter every Indian in Michigan was granted the right of citizenship." Julia was referring to the 1838 "Trail of Death," when Potawatomis in Indiana were forced on a two-month, nine-hundred-mile walk to Kansas.

Julia ended her talk by saying, "We are all brothers and sisters under one shepherd, and that the Great Spirit is God of all."

The tipi stood in a protective metal cage, as seen in this vintage postcard. *Courtesy of Ypsilanti Archives.*

After her talk, Julia designated EMU student Nettie Purdy as an honorary member of the Potawatomis and named her as official caretaker of the tipi. The ceremony's participants then set off on a tour of historic spots in Ypsilanti and of the site of a local section of the Potawatomi Trail that once wound along the north bank of the Huron River.

The birch-bark tipi was intended as a permanent memorial on campus, and a fence was built around it. Despite this protection, the structure suffered over time from exposure and a lack of maintenance. In 1919, the tipi was taken down and put into storage.

"Where Is the Wigwam?" asked a headline in the January 22, 1919 *Normal News* student newspaper. "The birch-bark wigwam, that for many years has held the place of honor in front of the Science building has been removed. It has not been destroyed, but its condition made it necessary to do something if it were to be kept intact. So it has been taken down and will be placed where the weather will not affect it."

Its fate thereafter is unknown to the writer. Long after the local disappearance of this remnant of Potawatomi culture, the Pokagon band of Potawatomis, with more than 4,500 members, continues to live in southwest Michigan, centered in Dowagiac.

The Farmer and the Poet

Well remembered are Robert Frost's three sojourns to the University of Michigan in the 1920s, as well as his house on Pontiac Trail, now at the Henry Ford Museum. Forgotten are the works of Ypsilanti poet-farmer William Lambie.

Lambie belonged to a generation earlier than Frost, but like Frost, Lambie had Scottish blood and took as his subject the natural world. Unlike Frost, he never left the occupation of farming or made much money. Lambie never won anything more for his verses than friends' approval, with one exception: a penny postcard that Lambie valued as priceless. The postcard came from another poet whom Lambie admired.

Lambie immigrated to the United States in 1839 at age eighteen with his parents and eight siblings from the Scottish village of Strathavan just southeast of Glasgow. The family settled in Detroit and then purchased a farm in Superior Township just north of Highland Cemetery.

William Lambie with his oldest daughter, Anna, and wife, Mary, in the background. *Courtesy of Ypsilanti Archives.*

"We bought the Moon farm, in the town of Superior, in June, 1839, and had a fair, square battle with privations, exile and penury for many a day," wrote Lambie in an essay; he read aloud from it years later at a Pioneer Society of Michigan meeting. "It was the half-way house between Sheldon's and Ann Arbor, and had a bar for the sale of whisky. Kilpatrick, the pioneer auctioneer, said we could make more money on the whisky than on the farm, but we preferred the plow to the whisky barrel." The family purchased 150 sheep.

Lambie's father soon tired of America and in 1854 immigrated again to Ontario with his wife and younger children. Other siblings settled in Detroit. Only Lambie's brother, Robert, stayed in Ypsilanti, where he worked as a tailor and later opened a clothing store and then a dry goods store. Robert also served on the city's first city council in 1858.

William remained on the old Moon farm. Anna, the first of his six children, was born in 1851 when William was thirty. In his diary entry for December 13, 1886, Lambie wrote, "Anna's Birthday—It was a cold dreary day when she was born when we only had one wee stove and one room 12 by 16 and our few potatoes all froze—poverty within desolation." William and his wife, Mary, wallpapered the inside of the house with newspapers in an effort to save the houseplants, but the plants froze.

William eventually built a larger house elsewhere on the farm and planted a grove of oak and apple trees nearby. By 1860, at age thirty-nine, he had five children ranging in age from two to nine and a farm whose value adjusted for inflation—in an era of cheap land—was $94,000, a bit better than many of his neighbors.

On his eighty acres he raised oats, beans, wheat, barley, corn, chickens and sheep. He also produced poems. In a May 15, 1876 diary entry, he wrote, "A sick sheep drowned—pulling the dirty wool off a dead sheep is not very conducive to poetry."

After William's failed attempts to have a poem published in *Harper's*, local newspapers began publishing his work. "My poem Auld Lang-Syne [is] in the *Commercial*," he wrote in his diary on May 26, 1877. This was a reworking of the familiar lyrics. William called it "A New Version of Lang-Syne." His introduction to the poem reads, "It is a great pity that ever the world-renowned song of 'Auld Lang-Syne' should become the song of the drunkard, to lead either drunken or sober men farther away from temperance and virtue, and down the shameful road of disgrace and ruin. If this new song of Lang-Syne is not as good poetry as the old one, it at least inculcates better morality."

The original song, of course, had been partially collected and partially composed by Robert Burns. Burns's January 25 birthday was one of two annual events Lambie faithfully noted in his diary every year. Yet the "Ploughman Poet," the "Bard of Ayrshire," was not Lambie's favorite poet.

A portrait from about 1875 of the Scottish-born poet-farmer. *Courtesy of Ypsilanti Archives.*

On February 1, 1886, Lambie wrote in his diary, "[Daughter Isabelle] and I drove up with old Frank the horse, to her School. Good sleighing—Had a note from my favorite Poet Whittier." John Greenleaf Whittier's note was published in the *Ypsilantian*, in an edition unfortunately not locally available on microfilm. It was one of two artifacts Lambie would receive from Whittier.

The Presbyterian Lambie shared several values with the outspoken abolitionist Quaker poet, such as pacifism. In Lambie's essay "Out in the Harvest Field," from his 1883 collection of prose and poetry *Life on the Farm*, he wrote, "We detest all kinds of war and battle and murder, and believe it is far more manly and heroic to fill a man's sack with corn than it is to kill him in battle."

Lambie was also sympathetic to the spirit of abolition. The other annual event he always noted in his diary was Emancipation Day on August 1, commemorating Britain's 1833 Slavery Abolition Act, which one year later ended slavery in most of the British empire. It was an antebellum holiday that was observed locally in Washtenaw County, Detroit and Ontario—Canada was one of the British possessions affected by the act.

In 1876, William attended the August 1 Emancipation Day celebration in Ypsilanti. In his diary, he wrote, "Ground very dry—hoping for rain—the colored man's day of Freedom—[Isabelle] and I went to see the Celebration

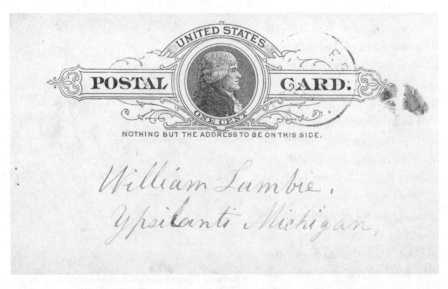

Lambie sent this self-addressed penny postcard to his idol. *Courtesy of Ypsilanti Archives.*

The reverse of Lambie's returned postcard, showing Whittier's handwriting. *Courtesy of Ypsilanti Archives.*

in William Cross Grove at the Fair Grounds [now Recreation Park]—The dark Beauties rigged out in white, red and blue and a feast of good things. Apples 75¢ a bushel."

In December 1887, at age sixty-six, Lambie wrote a poem to Whittier in honor of the poet's eightieth birthday. He enclosed a prepaid penny postcard. The return address, "William Lambie/Ypsilanti, Michigan," is written in Lambie's plain yet graceful hand. The Quaker poet returned Lambie's penny postcard.

On January 17, 1888, Lambie wrote in his diary, "Received a kind complimentary postcard from my favorite poet, Dear delightful John Greenleaf Whittier." Written in a rapid, looping script, the postcard reads, "Dear Friend, I heartily thank thee for thy poetical tribute and am thy sincere friend. John G Whittier."

Lambie saved this card and passed it down through family members. More than a century after Lambie's 1900 death and burial at Highland Cemetery, the tiny and delicate card continues to be cared for today. The fragile relic speaks to the heart of a down-to-earth Ypsilantian farmer who never pretended he was otherwise and yet befriended one of the nation's leading poets:

A family reunion at the Lambie farm homestead. *Courtesy of Ypsilanti Archives.*

When winter days grow dark and dreary
And I am sad, and weak, and weary,
His pure sweet lines oft make me cheery.
Even Milton in his strains sublime.
And Burn's in my land of Lang-syne
Are not read so well by me and mine…

—"Whittier," William Lambie

ABOUT THE AUTHOR

L aura Bien is a local history columnist for the *Ann Arbor Chronicle* and the *Ypsilanti Courier*, as well as a volunteer at the Ypsilanti Archives. Her areas of research interest include labor history, women's history and obsolete technology. She lives with her husband, Fritz, in Ypsilanti, Michigan.

Visit us at
www.historypress.net